Biofeedback

ROBERT M. STERN, Ph.D.

WILLIAM J. RAY, Ph.D.

Biofeedback

Potential and Limits

UNIVERSITY OF NEBRASKA PRESS
Lincoln and London

Bison Books in Clinical Psychology
George Stricker, General Editor

© DOW JONES-IRWIN, 1977

All rights reserved. No part of this publication may be reproduced, stored in a retrieval system, or transmitted, in any form or by any means, electronic, mechanical, photocopying, recording, or otherwise, without the prior written permission of the publisher.

First Bison Book printing: 1980
Most recent printing indicated by first digit below:
1 2 3 4 5 6 7 8 9 10

Library of Congress Cataloging in Publication Data
Stern, Robert Morris, 1937–
  Biofeedback.

  (Bison books in clinical psychology)
  Originally published by Dow Jones-Irwin, Homewood, Ill.
  Includes bibliographical references and index.
  1. Biofeedback training. 2. Medicine, Psychosomatic. I. Ray, William J., 1945– joint author. II. Title. III. Series.
BF319.5.B5S74   1980   615.8   79-18700
ISBN 0-8032-9114-0

This book originally was published under the title: *Biofeedback: How to Control Your Body, Improve Your Health, and Increase Your Effectiveness.*

Reprinted by arrangement with Dow-Jones Irwin

Manufactured in the United States of America

Preface

"Let your cancer disappear with image rehearsal and biofeedback." "Image rehearsal and biofeedback to let your joints be normal and comfortable if you have arthritis." "Feel wonderful without the urge to drink alcohol excessively with image rehearsal and biofeedback."

These are the titles of tape recordings being offered for sale by a company in California. With such claims being advertised it is no wonder that we frequently receive requests for information from people who hope to be cured through the use of biofeedback, or who would like to cure others of serious ailments with the aid of biofeedback. One of the biggest problems in the area of biofeedback is substantiating the "miracle" cures that have been claimed and are being used in advertisements by biofeedback therapists, biofeedback training schools, and biofeedback equipment suppliers.

The purpose of this book is to help you identify what is fact, fantasy, and fiction among all the information and misinformation being transmitted about biofeedback. Following introductory chapters in which biofeedback is explained and the procedures used are outlined, we present a description and evaluation of the application of biofeedback both to specific disorders such as migraine headache and to more general conditions such as pain and alertness. Concluding chapters summarize the present state of biofeedback, some aspects of its potential, and further information for those interested in pursuing its use.

We would like to thank Stephanie Knopp for the illustrations. Our thanks go also to our secretaries, Esther Strause and Ginger Swanger for typing the various revisions of our manuscript.

March 1977   **Robert M. Stern**
                                                                           William J. Ray

Contents

part one
Biofeedback: What Is It?

1. What Is Biofeedback? 3
2. Disease and Stress, 8
3. Biofeedback, Zen, Yoga, TM, Relaxation Response, and Autogenic Training, 14

part two
Biofeedback: How Is It Done?

4. Early Scientific Research, 29

part three
Biofeedback: What Has Been Done?

5. High Blood Pressure, 45
6. Heart Rate Disorders, 52
7. Raynaud's Disease: Cold Hands or Feet, 56
8. Asthma, 61
9. Epilepsy, 65
10. Tension Headaches, 70
11. Migraine Headaches, 76
12. Stomach and Intestinal Disorders, 80
13. Pain, 87

14. Bruxism: Excessive Teeth Grinding, 95
15. Muscle Reeducation, 100
16. Control of Paralyzed or Artificial Limbs, 107
17. Teaching Deaf Children to Speak, 113
18. Stuttering, 119
19. Alertness, 126
20. Lie Detection, 133
21. Creativity and the Human Potential, 140

part four
Biofeedback: Problems and Promises

22. Summing Up, 149

part five
Biofeedback: More Information

23. Sources of Additional Information, 159
24. The Instruments Used to Do Biofeedback, 162
25. Equipment Suppliers, 170

Glossary, 172

Notes and References, 178

Index, 193

part one
Biofeedback: What Is It?

1

What Is Biofeedback?

Could the autonomic (involuntary) nervous system be taught to learn through techniques that previously had been reserved for the central (voluntary) nervous system? This was the somewhat stuffy academic question of the 1960s which excited many psychophysiologists including us. Several years passed before the general public learned about biofeedback (a subarea of psychophysiology). And then it happened. Biofeedback emerged and the concept took a quantum leap in media coverage. Overnight there were institutes teaching mind control, businesses hiring consultants to teach their employees to be more creative through brain wave control, and full page ads selling biofeedback machines and publications extolling the wonders of biofeedback.

The term feedback was first used by the mathematician Norbert Weiner and defined by him as "a method of controlling a system by reinserting into it the results of its past performance."[1] Biofeedback, then, is a special case of feedback. Examples of feedback can be found in the normally occurring control systems of all living organisms. When a sleeping giraffe awakens, pulls his legs together and stands up, there is insufficient blood pressure to pump blood all the way up to his brain. Internal sensors detect this insufficiency and send out signals that bring about cardiovascular changes such as an increase in heart rate. These changes quickly bring about an increase in blood pressure and thereby an adequate amount of blood gets to the giraffe's brain and he doesn't get dizzy and fall over. You may have experienced a limitation of this same feedback system if you have ever leaped out of bed very suddenly and stood up straight. If you do this too quickly you may feel light-headed or dizzy, indicating that your postural change was so rapid that your internal blood pressure feedback mechanism couldn't keep up with you. In an extreme case you may actually fall down because of inadequate blood supply to your brain, but then you can start all over again, this time getting up more slowly.

Now what if you had a panel of lights that was connected to you in such a manner that as you stood up, it would reflect the amount of blood that your brain was receiving? Chances are, that if you had this information, you would not stand so quickly as to pass out and fall down. This would be one example of taking a biological response (the amount of blood going to the brain) and feeding it back to the person in the form of an external display. This procedure is what we mean by biofeedback.

"Biofeedback can be defined as the use of monitoring instruments (usually electrical) to detect and amplify internal physiological processes within the body, in order to make this ordinarily unavailable information available to the individual and literally to feed it back to him in some form."[2]

What Is Biofeedback Good for?

The primary function of biofeedback is to help us tune in to our bodies and in so doing reestablish the natural internal harmony that is synonymous with good health. Most of us are too busy these days to be good listeners. If we were psychologists who dealt with parent-child relationships, we would warn you that failure to hear what your children are trying to tell you can lead to serious juvenile behavior problems. As psychologists who study and treat psychosomatic disorders, we warn you that failure to hear the messages coming from your own body can result in disorders ranging from ulcers to migraine headaches to high blood pressure.

Let us use a hypothetical example of a person who complains of frightening attacks of heart palpitations; that is, his heart seems to pound rapidly in his chest. His experience can show how biofeedback can help an individual to reestablish internal harmony and good health. When Mr. R. first comes to see us he reports that he is not aware of his heart's beating except when he has an attack. He receives no signal from his heart. We have Mr. R. take off his shirt so that we can tape a small microphone to his chest. We then amplify the sound of his heart beating and permit Mr. R. to hear it over a speaker. He is now encouraged to relax and let his heart rate decrease. After a few minutes we tell him to think arousing thoughts and in so doing cause an increase in heart rate. We do this for 30 to 40 minutes twice a week for six weeks. By now

Mr. R. can make his heart rate go up and down at will. We might say that he has gained control of his heart rate to some extent. This is true, but we think a better way to summarize the important change that has taken place is to say that Mr. R. was tuned in to his heart rate. The next time he starts to have an argument with his wife over a trivial matter, he will listen to his heart, accepting the warning as he senses that it is speeding up, and back off from the situation in time to avert an attack. And when Mr. R. is working late at night to finish preparing his income tax return and his heart rate starts to go up, he will again listen to the internal signals that he now receives, get up and do something relaxing. Getting back in touch with your body is what we think biofeedback is all about.

Now that you know what biofeedback is and what it does you are probably asking why it has taken psychologists so long to apply it to human problems. Remember, most biofeedback work has been done since 1965. It turns out that psychologists and medical doctors had a theoretical bias against trying it. Their textbooks said it would not work.

What Changed Our Thinking?

What changed our thinking about how we might modify our internal bodily changes were two events that were happening at approximately the same time. The first event was the circulation in this country of reports about practitioners of certain Eastern disciplines who could voluntarily make changes in their physiological functioning. These reports ranged from stopping the beat of the heart to remaining buried for long periods of time without suffocating. In the 1950s and 1960s a number of teachers of yoga and other disciplines about which these claims had been made came to the United States. The presence of these teachers along with an openness of many in this country to hear what they had to say allowed for new theoretical possibilities.

The second event happened within the boundaries of traditional psychology. This was the development of new models, new ways of thinking about the body which could account for voluntary control of physiological functioning. One important model suggested that there was only one type of learning and that it applied to *all* of our bodily responses. This meant that researchers could begin to treat the previously considered involuntary functions of the body, such as blood pressure, in the same manner as they treated the voluntary ones such as raising your hand. The appearance of a new model is like the drawing of a map for an area that has not been charted before in that the model encourages a number of scientists to undertake studies that were previously not even conceived of. Thus, for the first time traditional scientists were able to study a person's ability to control his own body.

Before we examine specific disorders which are currently being treated with biofeedback, we will look at the general problem of disease and stress and then see how biofeedback compares with other nondrug, nonsurgical forms of treatment.

2

Disease and Stress

Most of us approach disease with the same ambivalence with which we confront death and dying. We view death and disease as something to overcome in a physical sense. For many people death and disease are merely problems of existence that with advances in science will go away. What do we really know about disease? In terms of descriptive definitions, we imagine we know much for we can name specific organisms that cause specific diseases. We can also describe the organic environment in great detail. But in terms of the process of disease, we must admit that we know very little. We don't understand, for example, the process through which a certain organism causes the disease, or why some individuals die from it while others seem to suffer only mildly. Specific research has led us into some curious findings. For example, if humans hold and touch rats that have been injected with cancer provoking substances, the held rats will develop cancer later than rats injected but not held. Also with certain types of mice, it has been shown that mice living together will develop cancer later than mice living alone.[1] What do these findings mean or better yet what is disease?

The Mystery of Disease

What is disease? We must admit it is still a mystery. We encounter some interesting paradoxes in our search for cures for our diseases. The first paradox is that as soon as one disorder is overcome, another comes forth to take its place. We have seen the plague of the middle ages decrease, only to be replaced with polio and then tuberculosis. In this century we have seen deaths from tuberculosis, pneumonia, and gastritis decline only to be replaced by deaths from heart disease and cancer. A second paradox is that as communicable diseases such as smallpox, polio, yellow fever and so forth have decreased, apparently noncommunicable disorders such as high blood pressure, ulcers, heart disease, and cancer have increased in number. A third paradox, and said by some to be one of the most closely guarded secrets of the medical profession, is that many disorders get better by themselves.

What can we make of all of this? Of the first paradox, we can say very little. We can just observe the disease statistics.

Stress-Related Disorders

Concerning the second paradox—that of a historical shift from communicable disease to more stress-related disorders—there are numerous theories that have been developed to account for this phenomenon. It has been suggested that as we have become more civilized, we have become more sanitary and thus reduced the prevalence of communicable disease; yet at the same time we have increased stress and thus stress-related disorders. Freud presented a picture similar to this when he suggested that the natural outcome of civilization is anxiety. Others have taken his lead and suggested that we no longer utilize our bodies in the manner in which they were designed to be used, and that this misuse leads to disease. That is, the cave man was able to feed himself when hungry, satisfy sexual desires when aroused, and so forth. Modern man on the other hand, does not listen to his instincts but is guided by the clock, his job, the freeway, picking up the kids at school, and so on. Although modern man has adapted his life-style to fixed schedules, his physiology may still be that of the caveman. If this is so then modern man experiences a split between what is going on inside his body in terms of normal physiological reactions and the patterns that his new life-style requires.

What does this conflict between physiology and life-style produce? Stress, anxiety, tension and disease (dis-ease) are the answers commonly given—with hypertension, heart attacks, and headaches being the specific disorders generally listed. How do these problems come about and is there anything that can be done about them?

"Wisdom of the Body"

Walter Cannon, who has shaped much of our thinking about the role of emotional excitement and its relation to physiological responding, suggested in the 1930s that our human body developed along the lines of a certain wisdom.[2] This wisdom, as Cannon called it, allowed the body to take care of itself with little requirement for "conscious control." For example, imagine yourself walking in the woods. It is a very calm, clear, and beautiful day. You are far into the woods and are overcome by the beautiful trees and flowers that you find along the way. Your mind wanders and you think about other pleasant experiences you have had in your life, when all of a sudden—in front of you stands a big black bear. What do you do? Well, before you have a chance to think about it, your body has already reacted to the situation. A gland called the adrenal medulla begins to secrete adrenalin. Adrenalin causes a rise in blood sugar by its action in conjunction with the sympathetic nervous system to release glycogen from the liver. There is now more sugar in the blood. The blood itself will be circulating differently since the heart will be beating faster, and more blood will be going to the brain and the muscles. Respiration will deepen and the oxygen interchange in the lungs will become greater. Also, those systems not needed to handle the emergency such as the stomach and intestines will decrease their rate of activity. Your time has come; the bear is ready to strike. You either run with the bear behind or fight. And at the completion of whichever action you select, if you survive, your body by the use of its homeostatic mechanisms returns to normal.

This situation (of a bear or other life or death experience) was faced daily by our ancestors. Cannon believed that our physiological responses developed in response to this type of emergency situation. This was the "wisdom of our body" as he called it. Included in this wisdom as Cannon saw it was the activity (run or fight) that utilized the energy produced and helped the body return to normal. Today we face a different world than that of our forefathers and it has only been recently that the real prospect of death has not been an everyday occurrence. Although we still face emergency situations which require large amounts of energy and quick judgments, the majority of emotionally arousing situations today do not have a concluding segment in which the energy created by the body is utilized.

Take the same scene as before. You are walking through beautiful woods and a bear appears in front of you. Just as your body reacts physiologically, you hear someone yell "cut"; the bear is led away and you realize you have just walked up to where someone is making a movie. What do you do? Well, you say to yourself something like, "Wow, that bear was just part of a film—am I relieved." However, your body has really pushed itself to be ready to fight or run and now it is just standing there, idling with the accelerator all the way to the floor. This is the situation of modern life as many researchers see it physiologically. Your body is constantly being stressed through deadlines to meet, important interviews to make, bills to be paid, and other events which seem, in your head anyway, as life and death matters. Whatever the emotional stress, your body is still preparing you to run or fight; and you seldom end up doing either one until the bill collector calls.

Although the body has the ability to return itself to normal (homeostasis) as Cannon suggested, both Hippocrates 2,400 years ago and Hans Selye recently have pointed out that with this return to normal there is an element of "toil" or general wear and tear on the body. Selye suggested that stress can build up over a long period of time and the body not quite return to normal with each episode until the organism is weakened and exhaustion sets in.[3]

Other researchers have suggested that repeated stress breaks down the normal homeostatic mechanisms and this allows certain organ systems to be over- and underproductive. For example, there are normally acid secretions in the stomach which do not damage the stomach lining. Yet occasionally in some individuals something goes wrong and the acid eats holes in the stomach lining—ulcers. How can stress be combatted and unnecessary but normal physiological reactions be reduced without returning to a primitive or wilderness life style?

The key at this time appears to be related to reducing the

physiological responsiveness of the person to everyday stresses while still allowing him or her to react appropriately in *real* life-and-death situations.

Cause of Disorders

The third paradox—that many disorders get better by morning—is the most interesting of all because it suggests that our bodies contain a way out of our problem of disease, or at least a way to work with nature to contain and heal our disorders. As you may have guessed, this is where biofeedback and certain other treatments come in, but first let us look at some more background information about disease and especially our theories about disease. Our theories have often been built around disease as the result of something coming from outside to infect us internally. Most individuals believe that it is the disease that causes the problems, yet as we shall see shortly, it is we ourselves who must take some of the responsibility for the resultant disorders. In the Middle Ages it was the devil. Later in this country, it was the witches that caused man's problems and recently our medical folklore tells us it is the germs that are at fault. Although it is certainly true that germs do affect us, it should be noted that germs do not affect everyone in the same way. Whereas one person may die, another may not suffer from any symptoms, yet both people made contact with a certain germ or microbe. It is becoming more obvious that there are psychological-social factors that interact with the mechanisms of the body or may themselves be the mechanism of the body to modify the body's reaction to germs.

Disease as a Lack of Communication

What has been lacking in previous views of disease is an involvement of the patient himself and an understanding that he or she may be the real active ingredient. For example, Lewis Thomas has suggested that disease may be understood best as a lack of communication, or bad communication.[4] He further stated that cells overreact as in the case of pneumonia in which many of the disease symptoms are really a violent reaction of the lung tissue itself or in the case of certain viral diseases of the brain in which the primary damage results from the brain's reaction to the virus.

If we are at the mercy of our own defense reactions, or our own Pentagons as Thomas has phrased it elsewhere, what can we do to control our communicating?[5] One answer would be to reestablish communication within that organism that we call our body on all levels. But, how? Well, there are a number of therapeutic approaches that have explicitly or implicitly set up the task of reintegrating the individual, at least on a psychological-physiological level, both to himself and to his world. Biofeedback is one such approach although a newcomer to this area. In the next chapter we will look at some of the other methods.

3

Biofeedback, Zen, Yoga, TM, Relaxation Response and Autogenic Training

> There is no better way of cultivating
> human nature and life than to bring
> both back to unity.
> *The Hui Ming Ching*[1]

Biofeedback may be seen as having three aspects. First, there are techniques for gaining control over one's physiological functioning whether it be heart rate, muscle tension, or brain waves. Second, biofeedback is a means of developing awareness of one's body and learning to recognize which aspects are related to various types of functioning. For example, you may learn to sense tension in your neck before it leads to a headache. And third, biofeedback requires a certain attitude in order to gain control over your physiological functioning. In this chapter we want to examine other techniques which have claimed also to give a person control and awareness of his physiology and to ask if there is an underlying similarity of attitude among the various techniques. Most of the methods that we will analyze have developed out of the meditative tradition. You must realize that presently we confuse the original goals of these techniques—such as higher consciousness or union with God—with certain aspects such as lower blood pressure or physiological control that have come to be associated with them today.

MEDITATION

Meditation, at least in the initial stages, may be seen as a process similar to biofeedback, but on an internal level. That is, the beginning meditator in Zen meditation is instructed to watch or count his breaths. In Theraveda meditation, the student is told to allow whatever processes or thoughts that come into his awareness to be the focus of meditation. In place of the external feedback concerning physiological functioning, the beginning meditator is instructed to tune into his own internal processes which may include the physiological ones. Awareness of physiology and other processes as well, were thought to be a by-product of meditation as opposed to the goal itself. In fact, so-called supernatural feats are often seen by experienced meditators as real blocks to continued development for they offer a distraction from the focus of meditation which is a reconnection of the meditator with the One, or God, or Reality or any of the many other terms that have been utilized to stand for the Ultimate Symbol.

Yoga

In general it has been the yogi who has received the most publicity concerning his ability to walk on hot coals, to be buried underground, or to stop his heart on command. However, upon close examination, it has been discovered that although these individuals may have remarkable control over their physiology, their claims—especially the ones describing direct mental control—were shown to result from a combination of respiratory and muscular control.

Elmer and Alyce Green at the Menninger Clinic in Kansas studied one such yogi who it had been reported could stop his heart.[2] Once the yogi was connected to the sensitive recording devices, it was realized that although he could reduce the pumping of blood, his heart actually didn't stop beating, rather just the opposite happened. The Greens tell of their work with Swami Rama as follows.

> The next day we hurried to the lab at nine o'clock (we had previously scheduled a lecture for him at ten o'clock) and wired him for the demonstration. Before starting his "inner focusing" procedure,

however, he said that when his heart stopped he wanted Alyce to call over the intercom from the control room and say "That's all." This would be the signal for timing the duration of his demonstration and would also remind him not to "go too far." He said that he did not want to interfere with the functioning of his "subtle heart," the one that lay behind the workings of his "physical heart." Having explained this, he made a few trial runs at speeding and slowing his heart, then said, "I am going to give a shock, do not be alarmed." To me this meant that he was going to give himself some kind of neural shock, but later I learned that he was going to shock the research personnel and doctors who were watching the paper records and polygraph pens in the control room, and they were being told not to be alarmed. After about 20 seconds of motionless silence I heard Alyce say, "That's all." At this, the Swami pulled in his stomach muscles for a few seconds, then he relaxed. From his look I could see that he felt the test had been a success, so I began asking questions about the "internal" process he used to accomplish such a thing. While he was answering, Alyce called over the intercom and said that the heart record was not what we had expected and suggested that I look at it before going any further.

To my surprise, the heart rate instead of dropping to zero had jumped in one beat from about 70 per minute to about 300 per minute. I returned to the experimental room and described the record to the Swami. He seemed somewhat surprised and bothered and said, "You know that when you stop the heart in this way, it still trembles in there," and he illustrated with fluttering hands. I speculated then that what we had recorded might be some kind of fibrillation, but later was told by Dr. Marvin Dunne, cardiologist and professor at the Kansas University Medical Center (Kansas City, Kansas), after he had examined the records, that it was a case of "atrial flutter," a state in which the heart fires at its maximum rate without blood either filling the chambers properly or the valves working properly. He showed me similar records obtained from patients and asked what happened to the Swami, he should have passed out; but I had to answer that we quickly "unwired" him so he could get to his lecture on time.

The atrial flutter actually lasted for an interval between 17 and 25 seconds. The exact duration could not be determined from the record because when the Swami drew in his stomach the resulting electrical signal from muscle firing caused the EKG pen to go off the edge of the paper, and after it returned the heart rate was normal again. I asked him why he had moved his stomach and he said that he had established a "solar plexus lock," by means of which the heart condition could be maintained for quite a long time if desired. It is interesting to note that when the heart began to flutter the people in the control room had a hurried consultation amongst themselves to decide if this was what the Swami meant by "stopping" his heart. After about eight seconds they decided that whatever it was it looked dangerous and decided to give the "that's all" signal.

Whereas the Greens waited for the yogis to come to them, some researchers in the late 1950s set out to find meditators in their normal place of abode, and also to discover what goes on during ordinary meditation if real meditation can be anything but ordinary. To find meditators meant that the scientists had to go to India and Japan. Although it is a humorous scene to imagine a group of scientists in white coats knocking on a cave to see if anyone was home, this is almost exactly what happened *sans* the white coats.

The work in India was performed mainly by M. A. Wenger of UCLA, and B. K. Bagchi of the University of Michigan Medical School with the aid of B. K. Anand of the All India Institute of Medical Sciences. What these researchers reported were the same findings the Greens of Menninger Clinic were to report some ten years later. Heart rate stoppage was not that at all but a reduction of blood flow in the limbs through the utilization of breath and muscle tension. Before you want to call these yogis fakers, it should be pointed out that they did have remarkable control over their bodies as was demonstrated by the ability of one of them to decrease his heart rate from above 60 beats per minute to below 30 beats per minute. But they don't *stop* their hearts![3]

Although checking out claims of yogis or even biofeedback machine manufacturers can be fun, it is also very necessary to ask how a person's physiology changes during periods of meditation and if you see differences between people who have been meditating for a long period of time compared with those who are just beginning. What Bagchi and Wenger found in India with 14 yogis was that in periods of meditation that ranged from 15 minutes to over two hours, there were trends toward stabilization or lowering of physiological activity.[4] Heart rate for most of the yogis did not change significantly during meditation. Respiration tended to

decrease. A rise in skin resistance, which is associated with relaxation, was also noted. The brain wave pattern was that of high amplitude alpha waves, 8-12 cycles per second, that is generally believed to represent a lack of activity in the brain. From these results Bagchi and Wenger concluded that the yogic meditative state is characterized by deep relaxation without drowsiness or sleep. Other research from India also reported a presence of alpha activity during meditation, and even in one case of two yogis who produced alpha waves while their hands were immersed in ice water for 45 minutes.

Zen

Research reported from Japan by Kasamatsu and Hirai in the mid 1960s looked specifically at Zen meditators and the effects of meditation on brain wave activity.[5] The report of this research suggested some interesting findings. First, in the Zen meditators the occurrence of alpha rhythms was very common whereas in a control group matched for age and who sat in a similar posture without meditating, alpha was not as predominant. Second, experienced meditators after a period of time began to show theta wave patterns, 4-7 cycles per second, which is the frequency range below that of alpha. Third, the Zen meditators did not habituate to a click when sounded many times whereas the control subjects did. That is, they responded to each click as if it was being heard for the first time whereas the control group stopped responding to it. This finding is particularly interesting since Yoga meditators had been shown to make no response at all to any outside stimulation. In this sense Zen and Yoga meditation did result in different physiological responding.

These results and a few laboratory experiments which examined how individuals could be taught to produce or stop alpha activity were all that the electronic counterpart of the fast food industry needed to turn to electronic yoga and instant enlightenment. The reasoning was as follows. If meditators have lots of alpha and meditation is good, then producing alpha will get the same results as meditation—only you don't have to wait for another lifetime or even 20 years to reap the results. However, fat people may sweat a lot, but sweating doesn't make you a fat person!

Transcendental Meditation (TM)

Adam Smith after making a sojourn into the world of those who claim to teach life, liberty, and truth reported back that Transcendental Meditation or TM as it is commonly called is the McDonald's of the meditation business.[6] By this he meant that they had taken a technique and packaged it and sold it similarly all over the world, even to keeping count of how many were sold. People who have been meditating in other systems for a period of time tend to look upon TM in the same way the scholars of the '60s looked upon free universities and liberal arts curricula without liberal arts courses. They felt that something important was missing. It is not that anyone says TM is wrong and in fact it is not difficult to obtain all the testimonials that one wishes for the benefits of TM. It is rather that the TM people took a process that had been previously kept relatively secret and required time and sacrifice to obtain and made it simple and available to anyone willing to pay the one time fee. The technique is simple. You sit for 20 minutes twice a day and say a word which is called a mantra over and over in your mind. Of course there is *more* to the four one-hour sessions that everyone world wide goes through than just being told one word and to sit twice a day in any comfortable position repeating the word. That more is what has made TM both Western in orientation and acceptable. That more is science. This has meant many articles in respectable scientific journals and even the granting of Ph.D.'s for further analysis of TM. One of the first dissertations was published by Robert Keith Wallace, then at UCLA.[7] Wallace's dissertation looked at a number of physiological measures including oxygen consumption, cardiac output, respiration rate, arterial blood pressure, EEG measures, CO_2 elimination, and heart rate while individuals performed TM. From his results he suggested that TM is a different state than waking, dreaming, or sleeping—that TM may produce a fourth state of consciousness. The general physiological pattern present in this and later studies indeed suggested a quieting of the nervous system. There is presently, however, considerable debate in scientific circles as to whether TM does really produce a unique state of consciousness.

RELAXATION RESPONSE

After performing some of the early research looking at the effects of Transcendental Meditation on physiological functioning, Herbert Benson decided that the apparently beneficial effects that were being observed with TM were not unique to it.[8] And in fact Benson went further to suggest that all meditation and other similar techniques had four ingredients in common, and if one would practice the four parts of what he called the relaxation response, then beneficial results would follow. Before we look at the four ingredients, let us reconstruct his reasoning.

Benson, as Cannon before him, suggested that the innate response of man, when faced with stress, is to prepare either to fight or to flee. The physiological side of this is an increase in heart rate, increase in breathing, increased blood flow, and an increase in blood pressure. As we mentioned previously, both Cannon and Freud suggested that we cannot in our civilized society either fight or flee. More often psychological adjustments to the situation are demanded. Thus we are left in a state of readiness or tension. Consider the boss calling you into his office, there is a rumor that someone is to be laid off. Your physiology is reacting and ready to respond. When you get to his office, you wait and your physiology continues to react, then he calls you in. He asks you a question concerning information about the number of stores in your district and then thanks you. Your head says everything is OK, but your body is still ready to run or fight. Benson believes, as we suggested in the previous chapter, that if fight or flight response is produced without being utilized appropriately, then heart attack or stroke may eventually follow.

The situation just painted is a bleak one. The head going in one direction and the body going in the other. Benson says that there is a way out. The way out is to reduce the tension in the body through what he calls the relaxation response. The relaxation response is made up of four elements:

1. A situation or environment that is quiet and without interference.
2. A word or phrase or sound that can be repeated over and over again.
3. A passive attitude (which Benson feels to be the most important of the four).
4. A comfortable position.

He suggests that this be practiced for 10 to 20 minutes once or twice daily.

Whether these four aspects are all that are needed to achieve health and well-being must remain an open question at this time.

However, it does appear that relaxation and passive rest during the day is as Benson suggests an aspect of our life that we have left out in our hurry to get where we are going. Benson is to TM as TM was to traditional meditation. To us, he reflects the American way, that is, to take the techniques of other cultures and to distill from them the main ingredients which leaves one with a technology. It is terribly American in that on the surface it appears neutral as has been the claim for all technology. There is, however, another aspect to the many meditative and religious procedures which Benson suggests can be reduced to the four steps of the relaxation response. This aspect is that these older procedures transmit with them a meaning or framework for understanding the outcome and the experience of the various techniques. It is true, as Benson has said, that we have left out the relaxation response in our hurry, but we have to ask *where* are we in a hurry to go?

AUTOGENIC TRAINING

Achtung! Relax. Ich bin ganz ruhig. Let it breathe you, or as is said in that language famous for box sentences where you have to wait ten lines to find out what you have just been reading is not true rather than true, "it breathes me." The language of course is German and the technique is that of autogenic training. The goal of a session of autogenic training is a state of light hypnotic trance, probably better understood as a type of autosuggestion or autohypnosis. The theory of autogenic training suggests that a state of relaxation induced through autohypnosis is incompatible to a state of tension. The technique itself which begins with the person saying to himself, "I am at peace," and then continues through a relaxation of different parts of the body was developed by Johannes Schultz in Europe. Schultz along with Wolfgang Luthe of Canada have suggested that the way to deal with tension and anxiety is not through so-called self-control for this just creates more tension, but through a type of passive concentration or relaxation which itself is antagonistic to the physiological and psychological state of tension.[9]

Probably the most important aspect of their work as a forerunner of biofeedback was not their search for methods of reducing tension but their desire to make the patient active rather than passive in the control of his own condition.

The method itself begins with the patient thinking a thought about a part of his body. For example, he would say to himself, "My legs are heavy." This was then followed by the self-statement, "My feet are warm." Schultz and Luthe equated heavy with relaxation and warmth with vasodilation. The person was to follow the basic procedure two or three times a day for an extended period of time.

By the end of three or so months the person who was practicing autogenic training had added to his list of statements and his period of passive concentration may have sounded as follows:

> I am at peace ... my arms and legs are heavy ... I am at peace ... heart beat calm and regular ... it breathes me ... my solar plexus is warm ... my forehead is cool.

Following this, standard meditative techniques such as visualization were begun. And in fact it has been suggested that experiences that one has in the advanced stages of autogenic training, such as seeing colors spontaneously and feeling as if you are floating, are also found in advanced stages of some meditative techniques.

Autogenic training has been utilized in conjunction with biofeedback by some clinicians as a means of directing attention and obtaining relaxation when a biofeedback instrument has not been available, such as in the patient's home, with positive results. Autogenic training like biofeedback aims at a general receptiveness of the person to himself.

CONCLUSION

How does it all work? The *Gita* suggests it is by nonaction.

> Abandoning attachments to the fruits of action,
>   Constantly content, independent,
> Even when he sets out upon action,
>   He yet does (in effect) nothing whatsoever.
>   *The Bhagavad Gita (Chapter 4, #20)*[10]

Although there are a multitude of techniques, the experience of many of the techniques of meditation, the relaxation response, autogenic training and biofeedback all suggest a common process. As suggested by the *Bhagavad Gita* in the above quotation the process is that which has commonly been called nonaction. However, to the Western man the term nonaction tends to suggest a cessation of all action which is not actually the meaning implied here. A better term for the Western man might be that of "allowing." That is, in biofeedback many researchers have reported that it is necessary to *allow* certain responses to come forth rather than to *make* them come forth. A clear example of this is relaxation. You cannot make yourself relaxed, you can only allow yourself to become relaxed. Joe Kamiya in his work on alpha training with biofeedback reported that individuals "who actively thought of what was going to happen next" were less able to produce an alpha state than those who were more passive and allowed the state to come forth.

Johannes Schultz and Wolfgang Luthe in their book on autogenic training suggest that we should make a distinction between active concentration which requires an effort in terms of attention and concern, and passive concentration which implies a casual attitude and basic passiveness in terms of how a certain activity may turn out. For example, when looking at a book of photography, you would perform the task differently if you were looking for a certain picture to show someone later than if you were just looking for recreation. Eric Peper has suggested that one of the best everyday examples of passive attention or what we are calling *allowing* is that of urination. That's right, urination. If you think about this for a second you will realize that the process of urinating is basically a very passive one, you just allow it to happen rather than actively making it happen. In fact, as we have all found from physical examinations in the doctor's office, the command to urinate or any attempt on our part to make it happen often has just the opposite effect. In this case, to do, it is necessary not to do.

Would a passive attitude toward life help us to be healthy? For years we have been taught that the most fit of the species are the ones that survive. What Darwin meant by this was not that the most fit individual but that the fittest species was the one to survive. What some people are now beginning to suggest is that the wisdom of the body, as Cannon put it, may not in every case lead to the health of the individual. That is, the natural response of the body to stress may itself lead to disease as suggested earlier by Lewis Thomas. Freud suggested that a similar process took place on a psychological level. For example, when someone says something negative about us, much of our energy is spent "defending" against the statement by either denying it, or getting mad at the person, or sustaining an inner dialogue about how dumb this person is and how he can't possibly be right. Often the person may leave and we still continue to defend against the statement in our head. All this is wasted energy. How can we not defend against both physical and psychological stress to an excess?

Selye presents two simple answers to this question.[11] The first is to know yourself—there is nothing to defend against if you know and understand yourself. The second answer is to know when and how your body surrenders to disease and stress. Everything may be better by morning, but you have to know when to go to bed first. Although these two responses seem simple, we are suggesting to you that they form the underlying structure of a number of therapeutic procedures including biofeedback. In this sense, biofeedback may be seen as awareness (know thyself) combined with an allowing attitude which facilitates the cure.

part two
Biofeedback: How Is It Done?

4

Early Scientific Research

In the development of every field there are those who present a general frame of reference or map for others to follow and there are those who attempt to test out the specifics of the map, and to ask the question, "Is this really a good map before me?" In the past two chapters we have been looking at some general maps or statements about health, healing, disease, and such holistic processes as meditation. In this section we are going to examine one method for testing the specifics of the map, that of science, and the scientific background that has led us to our present state of biofeedback practice. This will include an examination of some of the early basic research which sought to find out if individuals could learn to control specific body responses.

Since the 1960s there has been a unique coming together of individuals interested in learning theory, psychophysiology, clinical psychology, and psychiatry that has produced biofeedback as a field of accepted scientific research. Some of the first questions asked dealt with the method by which the autonomic nervous system, that part of the nervous system which has control over responses such as your heart rate, blood pressure, skin temperature, salivation, and the galvanic skin response, could be taught new responses. The speculation for centuries had been that this so-called involuntary or autonomic system was somehow inferior to the more "voluntary" central nervous system which includes the spinal cord and brain and controls the activity of our skeletal muscles. In technical terminology, it was suggested that autonomic responses had to be elicited rather than emitted, thus the technique of classical conditioning had to be applied if changes in this response system were to be made. The central nervous system on the other hand was considered under conscious control and thus, in technical terms, instrumental learning or operant conditioning must be applied, in that responses could be reinforced only upon their emission. The main point of this is to show you that there has been a scientific bias for years, as we mentioned in the first chapter, suggesting that different systems of your body must be communicated with differently.

Application of Miller's Theory

One of the first scientists to challenge the assumptions surrounding the autonomic nervous system was Dr. Neal Miller of Rockefeller University. For 35 years Miller studied various aspects of learning and it has been his work that has given biofeedback much of its theoretical base. After some years of what Miller describes as unsuccessful results, he and his graduate students in the 1960s were able to demonstrate that animals had some control over the so-called involuntary functions.[1] For example, Alfredo Carmona and Miller demonstrated that thirsty dogs could be taught to salivate if water was utilized as a reward for salivation. It was also demonstrated that the dogs could learn to decrease salivation, again if water was used as a reward for the response. Critics of this work suggested that the animals did not really learn to control their autonomic nervous system, in this case the salivary gland, but rather that they made some voluntary muscle response such as chewing which in turn caused the salivation.

In order to counter this alternative hypothesis, Miller and his students began to use a drug called curare in their animal research. The specific function of curare that made it ideal for the research Miller wanted to conduct is that it paralyzes skeletal muscles including the respiration function while still allowing neural control of the visceral organs and glands. An early study using curare in Miller's laboratory was performed by Jay Trowill. After immobilizing a rat and placing it on a respirator, Trowill and Miller found that if electrical stimulation was supplied to a pleasure center of the rat's brain following each heart rate change in the desired direction, the rat could be taught to either increase or decrease its heart rate. Over the next years and continuing to the present time, the work of Miller's laboratory has been directed at the theoretical questions surrounding whether animals can be taught to control responses previously believed to be totally "involuntary." The work to date suggests that highly specific control can be achieved by some lower animals and by humans.

The findings of this research are further supported by the work of Dr. Ádám in Hungary.[2] Dr. Ádám was interested in the question of why internal responses of an organism tend to remain at an unconscious level and further could these responses be brought into awareness. Ádám believed that human beings could learn to become aware of more internal sensations than just pain. To reach this conclusion, he had not only examined the requirements for bringing internal stimulation into consciousness for humans but had also shown that dogs could discriminate sensations in their intestine as small as two or three inches apart.

Electroencephalogram (EEG)

Another early researcher in that area later to be called biofeedback was Joe Kamiya.[3] Let us reconstruct one of his early studies. You are going to be part of the experiment. First you are told to sit down and relax and then electrodes are attached to your scalp so that the electrical activity of your brain can be recorded. This electrical activity of your brain or electroencephalogram (EEG) is then picked up by the electrodes on your scalp. The precise source within the brain of the EEG activity is not presently known, but we do know that it reflects the activity of millions of brain cells. Yet although we don't actually know what EEG does or what it is, we have made some associations between different brain activity states, classified by their amplitude and frequency, and certain activities. For example, when a person is thinking, the activity of the brain is generally of low amplitude and high frequency (13-25 cycles per second also referred to as 13-25 Hz.) and is known as beta activity, or beta waves. If a person sits quietly and relaxes, often a high amplitude and slower wave is present. This EEG activity is called alpha (8-12 Hz.). An even slower wave (4-7 Hz.) is associated with the onset of sleep and is called theta activity. See Figure 1 for an illustration of different patterns of EEG.

FIGURE 1

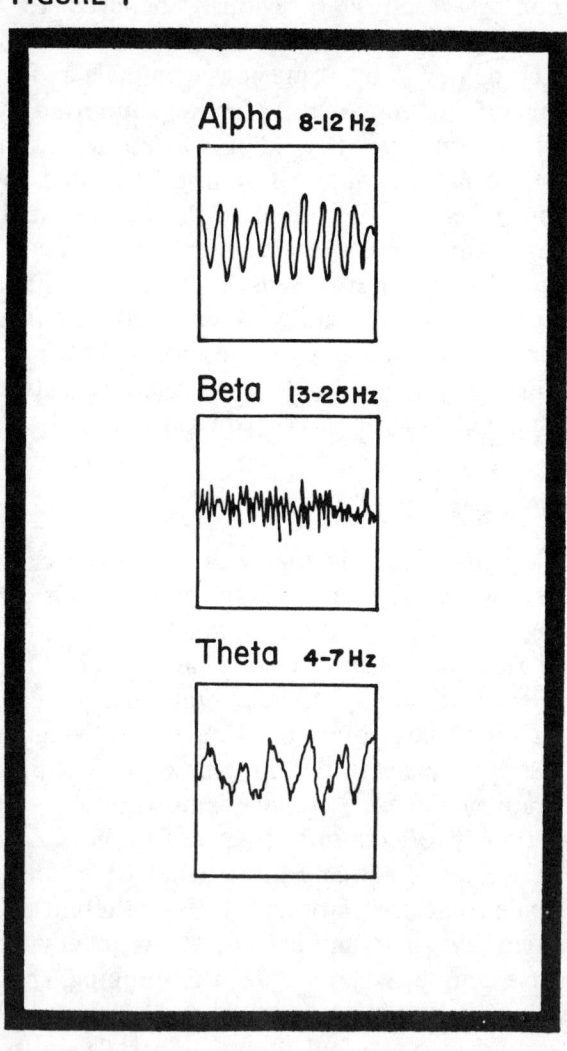

Dr. Kamiya's Research

Now back to Dr. Kamiya's experiment. You are told that the experimenters are interested in two brain wave states, one which will be called "A" and the other "B." You are also told that from time to time you will hear a bell and when the bell rings you are to signal whether you were in state "A" or "B." How do you do it and what do the two states represent? You don't know. After a period of time, guessing which is state "A" and which is state "B," you begin to have a feel for what the differences between the two states are. You can't quite verbalize it, but you are right in guessing whether it is state "A" or state "B." The difference between the two states you find out later was whether you were showing alpha activity in your brain or not. The work clearly demonstrated that individuals could learn to discriminate whether or not they were in an alpha state.

The next stage in Kamiya's research was to ask if you learn to discriminate whether alpha was present or not, could you also learn to control the presence or absence of alpha activity. To answer this question, Kamiya devised one of the first biofeedback studies. He designed his equipment so that every time a person was producing alpha activity, a tone would come on and when the alpha activity changed into beta, the tone went off. The task of the subject was thus to keep the tone on and this was accomplished by remaining in a state of alpha. The early results appeared clear. Some individuals could learn to control their brain wave activity in a surprisingly short time.

Controlling Alpha Activity

Now the interesting part. How did these individuals go about controlling their alpha activity? Most people couldn't tell you. It was a feeling but difficult to put into words. Joe Kamiya and others did realize however that most people went through a set of stages on their way to learning alpha control. At first most individuals actively "try" to control their alpha and this appears to produce just the opposite effect, alpha is inhibited. The second stage involves forgetting about the experiment and the desire to control alpha. At this point alpha seems to reappear and increase.

The person becomes relaxed. It is not the type of relaxation that puts you to sleep, but more like the process of nonaction or "allowing" that we discussed in the last chapter. This is the third and last stage in the development of alpha. It is reported as the feelings of being relaxed and alert at the same time. Since this sounds similar to the type of attention that some meditators talk about when they say that they just watch what is going on without interfering with it, it has been suggested that the alpha experience and meditation may be similar. But are they?

We must answer that we just don't know. In terms of meditation, we can say that individuals who have practiced meditation in various forms both in other countries and the United States show higher alpha levels during their meditation. However, we can in no way conclude, as some have wanted to do, that the active ingredient in meditation is alpha for there is also a reduction in the rate of respiration and an increase in the level of skin resistance along with other changes during meditation.

What can we say thus far about alpha control? First, individuals can learn to discriminate when they are in an alpha state and when they are not. Second, individuals can learn to block alpha, that is to reduce its production, and to increase alpha. And, third, alpha is in general associated with internal feelings of relaxation and pleasantness. We cannot however make any statement as to whether this state of relaxation is the result of the production of alpha or whether the increase of alpha is produced by relaxation. We can only say that the two seem to go together. Related to this, we also cannot say what the mechanisms are that produce alpha in terms of the physiology of the person.

It was noted that certain individuals have a high level of resting alpha, that is, their brain wave pattern has more alpha in it as compared with the general population. However, this high level of alpha appears not to give these individuals any advantage in learning, reading, or other abilities that are sometimes thought to be associated with alpha. In fact, some researchers have reported that they find individuals with high baseline alpha activity to be less interesting people to interact with in general.

With all the talk about biofeedback and especially alpha control, you might believe that we know much about alpha and its relationship to relaxation. We have all seen the advertisements in popular magazines that offer for sale "alpha machines." The implications from the ads are that being in alpha will help you study better, remember more, have better sex, sell more cars, be more relaxed, and so forth. The truth is that we know very little about what alpha activity is and how it relates to human functioning. As with many so-called scientific findings, there has grown up a cult of believers who have seized upon alpha training and imagined it offered them a shortcut to power, magic, and internal bliss.

Electromyogram (EMG)

Focus your attention on your forehead muscles; these are called the frontalis muscles. Feel the level of tension in them. Now, begin to think of something unpleasant or an event that you are not looking forward to. Could you tell when the muscles became tight? If you had been able to notice all of the activity of the muscles you would have seen that the thought itself brought about some tension and that it was some time before you consciously felt this increase in your muscle activity.

Every time a muscle contracts a small amount of electricity is given off, the amount being proportional to the degree of concentration. We can record this electrical activity, the electromyogram (EMG) in a manner somewhat similar to the procedure used for recording EEG. Two electrodes are placed over the muscle under study and the small signal is led via wires to an amplifier and then to a recorder. It should be noted that we can record the amplitude of your EMG even when the degree of contraction of your muscle is so slight as not to be detectable by someone staring at your nonbulging biceps.

This principle was used in an early application of biofeedback. A team of workers at one of the hospitals connected with Indiana University[4] was trying to deal with the problem of how to get children to exercise whose muscles had atrophied due to polio. The children had recovered from the disease and needed exercise to regain strength in their muscles, but most of them would not exercise. The basic problem was that when the children did try to flex their badly weakened muscles, nothing happened. They received no feedback. That is, in the early stages of their recovery each time they flexed their muscles, the muscle was slightly strengthened but not to the extent that the child could see or feel any change in performance. A psychologist had the original idea to record each child's EMG from the muscle under study and to use the amplified signal to light up a clown's face, a response the children found very rewarding. Most of the children gladly did their exercises. Without this special form of biofeedback the children would have had to exercise perhaps thousands of times until they would have received natural feedback (seeing or feeling their muscle getting bigger) and they probably would not have done it. You can now begin to see that with some types of feedback of your muscle activity, you could learn to discriminate in much the same way as the alpha subjects learned to discriminate far beyond their normal perception.

Muscle Potential and Biofeedback

Some of the earliest biofeedback work, although the word "biofeedback" was not known at the time, was with muscle potentials. As early as 1940 it was determined that an individual could learn to control single motor units. This research is particularly impressive since what we consider to be a muscle and muscle activity is made up of numerous single motor units.

An interesting application of this work is to be found in the early biofeedback research of Dr. J. V. Basmajian.[5] In this work, he examined individuals who played musical wind instruments in terms of the muscle activity of their lips and cheeks. He found that the pattern of the muscular activity was related to their ability to play the instrument. What he is now trying to do is to determine if he can teach—through biofeedback techniques—less skilled musicians the patterns of more skilled ones in hopes that this will in turn affect their playing ability.

Another area of research has focused on the activity of entire muscles or muscle groups, especially in relation to tension. Much of the early work in this area has been performed by Stoyva and Budzynski.[6] In preliminary work it was found that if you relax the frontalis muscles, this would aid in achieving a general relaxation of the entire body. In a series of studies it was determined that individuals who received feedback learned to relax faster than individuals who received no feedback. It was also found that an individual can be taught progressive relaxation by setting the feedback level at a lower level of muscular activity during the training. That is, in the beginning of the training, the person would be given feedback that he was doing the task correctly for a small decrease in muscle tension. Later on, he would be required to decrease his muscular activity to a lower level in order to obtain the feedback. This type of shaping procedure, which we have seen used in previously discussed studies, allows the person to learn at his own rate.

Since some psychologists have argued that relaxation and anxiety are incompatible, it was suggested that biofeedback might offer an effective technique for training in relaxation. Biofeedback would then be combined with traditional clinical techniques with the goal being more efficient treatment. We will discuss some of the current applications of muscle feedback to such problems as headaches and bruxism (excessive grinding of teeth) in later chapters.

Galvanic Skin Response (GSR)

In the early 1960s, Stern began a series of studies concerned with the ability of subjects to control voluntarily the frequency of their galvanic skin responses (GSRs). A GSR is defined as a decrease in skin resistance which is generally measured from the hand. GSR was selected for investigation rather than some other autonomic nervous system response primarily because Kimmel[7] had recently reported that the GSR could, contrary to what learning theorists had told us, be operantly conditioned in the same manner as central nervous system responses.

In the first of a series of studies, Stern[8] had college students try to increase their GSRs for ten minutes and decrease them for ten minutes. All subjects were told what a GSR is and that they could produce them by thinking arousing thoughts and suppress them by thinking relaxing thoughts. They were cautioned not to breathe irregularly or use muscular activity to produce the desired response. Half the subjects were allowed to watch their responses on a meter and half received no feedback. The individual results indicated that some subjects could produce GSRs when so instructed but could not suppress them during the "decrease" period, some could not produce GSRs at all and some could increase and decrease the frequency of their GSRs at will. The group results indicated that without feedback the majority of subjects could not produce GSRs after the first minute or two. The majority of feedback subjects, on the other hand, were able to keep making GSRs during the entire ten minutes.

The importance of feedback had been demonstrated for one session, but what would happen if subjects were brought back for several sessions? A new group of college students was studied using the same procedure as above except that they returned for four sessions. Subjects who received no feedback showed a much lower level of control of their GSR than the feedback subjects during the initial session, and more important, they showed no improvement over sessions. The feedback subjects performed at the same level for three sessions and then showed a significant improvement during the fourth.

It was decided to locate and study a group of people who would have had considerable practice controlling their emotions to see if such practice would aid them in controlling their GSRs. A group of professional actors was studied to see if they could, indeed, increase and decrease the frequency of their GSRs at will.[9] The procedure was similar to that described above except all subjects received feedback. The actors were divided into two groups: method actors and nonmethod actors. Method actors express emotions on the stage by thinking of a personal experience from their past that included the desired emotion. The appropriate bodily changes follow, for example, crying. The nonmethod actor, on the other hand, expresses emotion by changing his voice or expression but doesn't experience the actual bodily change of the character being portrayed. The results showed that method actors could turn their GSRs on and off at will while the performance of the nonmethod actors was no better than that of the college students. Perhaps method actors simply are better at expressing emotion on the stage. Three professional directors were asked to rate each of the actors in the study on their ability to express emotion on the stage. There was no difference in the ratings for the two groups. These findings were interpreted to mean that practice in thinking about personal emotional events greatly enhances one's ability to control his GSR. Method actors had the relevant training and nonmethod actors did not.

At the same time that Stern was studying the ability of actors to control their GSRs in this country, Simonov was investigating the phenomenon in the Soviet Union and Brener was studying the ability of actors in England to control their heart rate. Simonov[10] trained two actors over many sessions in order to demonstrate the degree of control that can be achieved. In addition to being trained to control their GSRs with feedback the men were taught Morse code. By the end of the experiment the men could make large (dash) versus small (dot) GSRs at will and in so doing communicate with one another.

Controlling Heart Rate

Just as investigators who conducted the early studies of voluntary control of GSRs were stimulated by the pioneering GSR conditioning studies of Kimmel, the first psychologists to investigate voluntary control of heart rate were stimulated by a unique conditioning experiment conducted by Shearn.[11] Shearn found that the number of momentary increases in heart rate went up when they enabled the subject to avoid an electric shock. Subsequent reexamination of Shearn's data revealed that in some cases subjects were using respiratory changes to produce heart rate increases. However, what was important was that other investigators had started to think that if the heart rate response could be instrumentally conditioned, perhaps with the aid of biofeedback it could be brought under voluntary control. Two of the earliest demonstrations of voluntary control of heart rate with the aid of biofeedback were conducted in the laboratories of Lang[12] and Brener.[13] In the former study, subjects learned to control the variability of their heart rate while observing a visual display of their heart rate. In the latter subjects learned to increase and decrease their heart rate under biofeedback conditions.

Chalmers and Stern[14] were interested in the extent to which the effects of heart rate biofeedback would still persist after the feedback was removed. In other words, what will happen to the individual's heart rate when he leaves the laboratory and no longer receives biofeedback. Three groups of subjects were used in a heart rate control experiment which was divided into two parts. One group received continuous feedback (they observed their heart rate on a meter) during both halves of the experiment, a second group received feedback only during the first half of the experiment, and a third group received no feedback. The interesting question was, will the performance of the second group during the second half of the experiment (when they received no feedback) be more like the continuous feedback group or the no-feedback group? The results indicated that their performance was more like the continuous feedback group. That is, during the second half of the experiment when they were no longer receiving feedback they still could control their heart rate, indicating transfer of training from a feedback to a no-feedback situation. This, of course, was an important finding for any clinical work with biofeedback.

Heart Rate and GSR

In a second experiment conducted as part of the same study the question of response specificity was investigated. That is, if we provide you with feedback from one response system, for example, heart rate, and tell you to increase your heart rate, will other autonomic nervous system-mediated responses, for example, GSR also increase? Heart rate and GSR were both recorded continuously from all subjects during both periods of the experiment. Half the subjects first received heart rate feedback and tried to increase their heart rate and then received GSR feedback and tried to increase that response. The other subjects performed the same tasks in the reverse order. All subjects were told that they could accomplish their tasks by thinking about emotional events. The heart rate and GSR responses were correlated to see if GSR increased for a given subject at the same point in time when heart rate increased and vice versa. The results indicated that there was not a significant correlation between the two responses, leading to the conclusion that biofeedback of a single response can result in response specificity.

The above finding was considered to be somewhat surprising. It indicates that with the aid of feedback subjects can find thoughts, images, and so forth, that cause their heart rate to increase without increasing their GSRs. Perhaps we should not have been so surprised when one considers that heart rate is primarily controlled by the parasympathetic branch of the ANS and GSR by the sympathetic branch. In other words, the two responses selected for study are really quite independent. But what about two responses that are very much related physiologically such as heart rate and blood pressure? Is it possible to train subjects to make one go up while the other goes down? Schwartz[15] performed such a study and provided his subjects with feedback and a monetary reward. He found that subjects can learn to integrate their heart rate and blood pressure (increase or decrease both jointly) and to a lesser extent differentiate them (increase one while the other decreases).

As was pointed out above while discussing control of GSRs, some subjects can control their heart rate to an almost unbelievable degree. Stephens, Harris, and Brady[16] worked with four subjects who demonstrated this ability. Their subjects were asked to control their heart rates by "pure mental means." They were given visual and auditory feedback of their heart rates and were paid according to their success. Whenever a red light came on they were told to increase their heart rate and when a green light came on they were to lower it. Each subject was given several trials. What follows is a summary of each subject's ability to control his heart rate (vary it in the correct direction from his resting level) by the final trial. Subject A could increase 24 beats per minute (bpm) and decrease 22 bpm. Subject B had a very low resting level (48 bpm) and so he was only trained to increase his heart rate which he did by 34 bpm. Subject C increased 15 bpm and decreased 6 bpm. Subject D also had a low resting level. He was only taught to increase; his heart rate went up by 29 bpm.

Why are some individuals able to play their internal organs so much better than others? We don't really know at this time. Stern and Kaplan, following their initial experiment on voluntary control of GSRs, gave each of the subjects several personality tests in an attempt to find differences between those who could and those who could not control their GSRs. The only test that seemed to discriminate between the groups was a test of sociopathy. The higher a person's score, or the more sociopathic, the poorer he did while trying to control his GSR. Very briefly, a sociopath is a person who experiences little guilt, or remorse, regardless of whatever actions such as lying or stealing he commits.

Ray[17] examined another personality measure, locus of control, in an attempt to learn more about individual differences in ability to control heart rate. Locus of control is a personality construct developed from social learning theory. It states that the effects of a reward on preceding behavior depend in part on whether the individual perceives the reward as being contingent on his own behavior (internal) or due to chance (external). Are you the master of your own fate or the victim of chance? Rotter, the man who developed the scale used to measure locus of control, suggested that the feeling that one can control his environment may be related to the feeling that one can control himself. Ray decided to test this. If Rotter's idea was correct then we should find that the internal locus of control people would be better able to control their heart rate as compared to the external locus of control people. When Ray looked at his results he found that they were not as straightforward as predicted. He found that the internal locus of control subjects were indeed better able to increase their heart rate. However, the external locus of control subjects were better able to decrease their heart rate. He then performed the experiment again with a larger group of subjects and found exactly the same results. Now, what did these results mean?

First, these results suggest that an individual's physiological functioning may be related to his cognitive style or the manner in which he approaches life. Second, these results demonstrate that every individual does not have the same ability to make changes in his physiology when requested to do so. And, third, from both the heart rate changes and self-report questionnaires which Ray gave his subjects it appears that individuals respond differently to the task of controlling heart rate and that these differences may be observed between groups identified by personality measures. This last implication suggests that biofeedback methodology may be applied to better understand psychosomatic medicine (the relationship between the psychological and the physical components in disease). The basic research we have briefly presented is only a small part of a large and growing body of evidence that points out our ability as humans to communicate with ourselves and to direct our body in ways we never considered possible before. Others such as Gerald Jonas in his book *Visceral Learning* and Barbara Brown[18] in her book *New Mind, New Body* have told the exciting story of the development of biofeedback in much more detail than we have here. At this point we want to turn our attention to the clinical applications of biofeedback to specific disorders.

part three
Biofeedback: What Has Been Done?

5

High Blood Pressure

Remember the last time that your blood pressure was taken at the doctor's office? How did you feel sitting in the waiting room? Did you feel some anxiety or a little tension? Most people do. With many doctors, after you have waited in the waiting room, you wait again in another room. What do you think about? Does this have anything to do with your blood pressure reading that is about to be taken? The data suggests that it does. Studies suggest that blood pressure readings taken in the doctor's office with the doctor present will be higher than blood pressure monitoring performed in a person's home.[1] The exact reason for this we do not know. One possible explanation is that the excitement of going to a doctor and then the waiting may cause temporary blood pressure increases. This is why many physicians accept a reading of high blood pressure only after a number of office visits, during which blood pressure can be monitored over a period of time. Consistent with the role of anxiety in producing high blood pressure are the studies which have looked at individuals under stress and found that often once the stress was removed the blood pressure would drop. For example, soldiers during battle periods have higher blood pressure readings than normal. After they left the front lines their pressure would again drop to normal. What all this leads to is that blood pressure should be seen as a measure which may vary both because of psychological factors and because of measurement factors. Of course neither of these factors suggests that blood pressure measurements should be ignored or their importance minimized.

Is Blood Pressure Important?

What else can we say about blood pressure in general? First, blood pressure appears to increase with age. The older you are, the higher your blood pressure will tend to be. Second, the average blood pressure found in one region of a country may be higher than that found in other geographical regions of the same country only miles away. Some of the counties of the British Isles demonstrate this regional variation with distances as close as 15 miles. Why should the region that one lives in be important in relation to high blood pressure? There have been a number of theories. Some researchers have suggested that diet is what is important. For example, in societies with a low salt intake, hypertension (high blood pressure) is uncommon, whereas groups that have high salt intake also show a higher incidence of hypertension. Although there is sufficient evidence to suggest a high correlation between salt intake and hypertension, there are exceptions to this rule. For example, Thai farmers whose intake of salt is double that of the U.S. average seldom develop hypertension. If blood pressure is as variable as it appears and changes with age or the region in which you live, is it really that important?

The answer to that question is yes in that hypertension has been found to be associated with higher risks of developing other disorders. One of the most famous studies examining this relationship is the Framingham study conducted over a long period of time in Framingham, Massachusetts. In this study a section of the general population was chosen and then these individuals were studied for developments which led to various diseases. This study along with similar ones that have been performed throughout the country have suggested that hypertension is one important factor associated with coronary heart disease, and other related problems such as arteriosclerosis and strokes.

Cause of Hypertension

Now that we know hypertension is important, do we know what causes hypertension? The answer is no. Recently, however, some researchers have begun to examine the variables associated with being hypertensive. Biochemical research has been one such avenue and our view of the causes of hypertension have been shaped by this. We are told that such diet factors as salt, fats, proteins, alcohol, and caffeine may play a role in high blood pressure although there appears to be an exception for every general rule that we discover in this area. Herbert Benson in his book, *The Relaxation Response,* suggests the importance of stress as a factor in high blood pressure. Some researchers have argued that it is stress that produces the elevated blood pressures in people migrating from more rural countries and occupations to those of a more industrial area. American Indian and Polynesian migrants both show an increase in blood pressure when living in more urbanized areas than when living in their traditional homes. However, when someone changes location, a number of other factors such as diet and activity level are often changed in the process. Some new evidence tends to suggest that it is not the move itself that causes hypertension. For example, new migrants do not show elevated blood pressure levels but their children who are born in the new land do. This has suggested to some researchers that hypertension or the predisposition for it may develop in childhood and only appear later in response to a number of variables.[2]

If the reason that a person has high blood pressure is unknown, that is, it cannot be attributed to either an endocrine or kidney disorder, then this condition of high blood pressure is referred to as "essential hypertension." Essential hypertension means only that the person has elevated blood pressure. Because persons with high blood pressure have been shown to have higher incidence of other diseases, most physicians believe that steps should be taken to keep pressure within normal ranges. Medication is the most popular means of blood pressure control utilized in this country.

Since medication has some undesirable side effects and since it has been demonstrated that psychological factors may themselves play a part in the elevation of blood pressure, researchers have sought to find other treatments for hypertension. These alternative forms of treatment include meditative-like procedures such as transcendental meditation and Benson's relaxation response. Biofeedback is also being explored as a treatment procedure.

Before you run down to your local biofeedback practitioner, we must warn you that there are many problems connected with blood pressure biofeedback procedures. One of the largest problems is the manner in which blood pressure readings are taken. A cuff is placed over your arm and the examiner listens with a stethoscope to the sounds of blood flow in the artery below the cuff, which are inaudible when the cuff is not tightened. If however the cuff is tightened so as to cut off blood flow and then slowly released, there is a faint sound heard. The first hearing of a sound with the stethoscope is used as the point at which systolic pressure, the highest pressure, is recorded from the cuff. As the pressure in the cuff is released, different sounds are heard with the stethoscope until no sound at all is heard. This in general is the point at which diastolic pressure, the lowest pressure, is recorded.

This procedure is not only distracting for someone attempting to perform a biofeedback task, but it also causes changes in the blood pressure itself. That is, just taking blood pressure over a period of time can cause a lowering of blood pressure which some attribute to the weakening or stretching of the artery under the cuff. Terry Kimper, working in our laboratory, and others are testing an alternative method for measuring something equivalent to blood pressure which will not require a cuff. His preliminary efforts have been quite successful and he is now planning to use this new indirect method of recording blood pressure in a biofeedback situation.

Treating Hypertension with Biofeedback

There are some very important beginnings where researchers and clinicians have attempted to apply biofeedback to the treatment of hypertension. Based on animal work where it was demonstrated that animals could be taught to either raise or lower blood pressure, the first question to be asked was, could anyone, especially individuals who did *not* have hypertension, be taught to decrease their blood pressure. One study of this type was performed by Shapiro, Tursky, Gershon, and Stern and published in the journal *Science*.[3] In this study men who were not hypertensive were given feedback in the form of a light and a tone for changes in systolic blood pressure. Their data indicate that men can learn to decrease systolic blood pressure under certain conditions.

The next step was to determine if hypertensive patients could also learn to lower blood pressure. This study was performed by Benson, Shapiro, Tursky, and Schwartz and published in 1971, also in *Science*.[4] These researchers studied seven individuals who had been diagnosed as having essential hypertension. The patients were first given a series of sessions in which their blood pressure was recorded but no biofeedback was utilized. Following these sessions, the patients were given daily hour-long training sessions in which biofeedback was utilized. After 8 to 13 daily sessions of feedback, the researchers reported that five of the seven patients had shown a considerable decrease in their systolic blood pressure in the range of 13 to 34 millimeters of mercury, the standard measure of blood pressure.

What happens outside of the laboratory and the biofeedback situation? In one case a biofeedback experiment played an interesting role in causing an individual's blood pressure both to go down and to go up. In this case reported by Gary Schwartz, a man was paid a certain amount of money for decreasing his blood pressure.[5] During the week he performed the task well enough to earn money yet the experimenters noticed that his blood pressure was always up again on Monday morning. After some discussion with the man it was learned that he took his money from the biofeedback sessions and went to the race track on the weekends. Of course the excitement of the races and losing money sent his blood pressure back up and him back to the experiment on Monday. This only suggests that no amount of biofeedback can change a person's life-style until they are willing to become involved in their treatment.

Assuming that the man and the race track was a somewhat special case, the next question that you must be asking yourself is does the lowered blood pressure from a biofeedback session continue after the biofeedback training session is over? That is, for biofeedback to have practical rather than just theoretical importance, it must be demonstrated that the patient's blood pressure does not return to abnormal levels after the training session is over. The answer to this question is a mixed one. Neal Miller reported an attempt to train essential hypertension patients to reduce their diastolic blood pressure.[6] According to Miller a few of the patients were able to reduce their systolic blood pressure, although he did not consider this to be successful training since the pressure began to drift back up again after reaching a lower plateau. There was one patient, however, who was able to make blood pressure changes. This woman, partially paralyzed from a previous stroke, was able with training to make blood pressure changes over a range of about 30 mm. Hg (millimeters of mercury). More important was the finding that her baseline blood pressure decreased from 97 mm. Hg to 76 mm. Hg by the last month of training. This woman appeared cured, yet unfortunately through what Miller refers to as an unusual combination of emotional stresses, this woman's blood pressure again increased. All was not lost though, for when the woman did return to biofeedback training 2½ years later, she rapidly regained a large measure of voluntary control.

A similar case report is from another biofeedback researcher, David Shapiro, who is presently at UCLA. Dr. Shapiro reported the case of a 35-year-old man.[7] This man was employed as a mental health worker and was both cooperative and motivated for biofeedback training. He had been diagnosed as having essential hypertension with a blood pressure reading of 160/110 mm. Hg (systolic pressure = 160 millimeters of mercury and diastolic pressure = 110 mm. Hg). Initially the patient was given biofeedback training during which time his diastolic pressure was reduced to about 85 mm. Hg. Further training in other procedures including autogenic techniques, and a form of relaxation training resulted in the patient's diastolic pressure ranging from 85 to 95 mm. Hg. His systolic pressure had dropped by the final session to between 130 and 135 mm. Hg. Following these nine sessions of biofeedback, the patient returned to his physician for another examination. His blood pressure at this time had again returned to 160/110 mm. Hg. Whether we should conclude that biofeedback was not effective or that his physician constituted a temporary stress situation that increased his blood pressure is not clear at this point. We can say that individuals at least in these two cases have been able to learn to decrease blood pressure through biofeedback, but also we must conclude that the training did not have a permanent effect.

A recent study with five hypertensive patients has reported more promising results.[8] In this study performed by Donald Kristt and Bernard Engel five patients who had been treated for hypertension for at least the past ten years were given biofeedback training. In order to assess the effects of the biofeedback training, these researchers first recorded blood pressure from their patients for a period of seven weeks. Following this the patients were trained both to increase and decrease blood pressure using biofeedback procedures. By the last week of training Drs. Dristt and Engel report that all patients were able to control their systolic blood pressure, some better than others. Follow-up work demonstrated that not only were the patients able to retain the ability to control blood pressure after one and two months of no training, but that blood pressures taken by the patients in their homes were also lower.

Now what can we say about biofeedback blood pressure training? The first statement we can make is that it is possible through biofeedback to make changes in either systolic or diastolic blood pressure in a laboratory setting even if you are suffering from essential hypertension. The second statement is that in the case of essential hypertension, the lowering of blood pressure which is achieved in the biofeedback training session may not continue into stressful encounters in everyday life. Before biofeedback can be considered the treatment of choice for hypertension, it is clear that more long term research must be performed.

6

Heart Rate Disorders

The heart is an organ that has throughout history caught our attention.[1] In Shakespeare we read that "a good heart's worth gold." Going back to Plato and Aristotle we find references to the heart as the center of emotional life. Even today we discuss someone emotionally in terms of the heart when we call a person "coldhearted" and "heartless" on the one hand and "warmhearted" and "full of heart" on the other. Thus, our common mode of speech today has not "lost heart" so to speak, although our present day physiology and medicine has reduced the role of the heart to that of an intricate pump. Modern medicine has focused on the mechanical properties of the heart, particularly the rhythmicity and conductivity.

Since the beginning of this century it has been believed that the initial heart impulse which causes the heart to "beat" begins in a region of the heart referred to as the sino-atrial node (S-A node). An electrical impulse then travels through the heart muscle which in turn causes the heart to contract and to pump blood. The demands on the heart by the body are very exact. The entire heart must contract more or less simultaneously while at the same time allowing for minute delays (100 milliseconds) at various points on the heart which allows for more efficient pumping. There is a wide range of disorders which reflect some problem in one of four areas concerning cardiac functioning which collectively are referred to as cardiac arrhythmias. These four areas are either

(a) an impulse is not formed properly at the S-A node, (b) the impulse does not spread across the heart properly, (c) the rhythm of the heart is out of line, or (d) the rate of the heart is not within normal limits.[2]

Some researchers consider the application of biofeedback to cardiac arrhythmias as one of the more convincing examples of the therapeutic effectiveness of biofeedback. The majority of this work has been performed in the laboratory of Dr. B. T. Engel in Baltimore. The work of Engel and his colleague has focused on a variety of cardiac disorders, one of which is characterized by premature ventricular contractions, called PVCs. The problem of premature contractions is that they occur before the time required for the ventricle, the main chamber of the heart, to fill with blood and thus result in inefficient functioning. These premature contractions—sometimes found in persons with certain types of heart injury—have been associated with sudden death and coronary artery disease.

Let us examine the manner in which Engel and his colleague Ted Weiss trained patients to reduce the number of PVCs.[3] The experimental procedure took place in two phases. In the first phase, the patients were trained either to increase or decrease their heart rate. Feedback was in two forms. The first form was binary presentation which consisted of a small yellow light which came on whenever the patient was able to change his heart rate such that it increased or decreased as instructed. For example, if the patient was instructed to increase his heart rate, then each time that his or her heart rate was above its normal level then the yellow light would come on. In this way the patient could come to learn what responses would increase heart rate and which would decrease heart rate. The second type of feedback utilized was a meter which displayed the amount of time that the patient was performing the task as instructed. For example, if he or she was instructed to increase heart rate, then the meter would turn on when the patient was performing correctly and would turn off when the patient was performing incorrectly.

In the second phase of the experiment, Weiss and Engel looked at the more clinically relevant phenomenon of heart rate range or variability. This measure was important since if a patient had a premature contraction, then the heart rate would appear to increase on the equipment. Following this increase from the premature contraction there would be a pause which would appear on the equipment as a heart rate slowing. Thus if a patient could be taught to keep his heart rate within a certain range on the equipment, then this would mean that he or she would be producing fewer PVCs than normal. The feedback display for controlling range was similar to that for the increasing and decreasing sessions. A yellow light was still utilized to tell the patients if they were performing correctly. However there was also a red light which came on if the patient's heart rate went above the normal range and a green light which came on when the heart rate went below the normal range. Thus, a PVC would appear to the patient as a red light flash (because the impulse came too fast) followed by a green light flash (the pause which follows a premature contraction). In this manner the patients were able to detect immediately when a PVC had occurred. In essence, then, the patients in the Weiss and Engel study were receiving feedback about what a PVC sequence was like and also the feelings and thoughts associated with keeping their heart rate within a normal range.

After a large number of training sessions, five of the eight patients were able to reduce PVCs with training in the laboratory and four of the eight showed evidence that the training was carrying over to periods outside the laboratory. One factor that may have helped the transfer of the learning outside the specific laboratory situation was that these researchers attempted to wean the patient from the biofeedback equipment by slowly reducing the number of trials in which the feedback was present. That is, over a period of time the patient was still instructed to keep his or her heart rate within a given range but feedback was not given on each trial as to how well the person was performing the task. These researchers hoped that in this way the patients could learn internal cues as to whether a PVC was present or not. In the follow-up work on one of the patients Engel reported that five years after the training, PVCs were rare and that she was not required to take antiarrhythmic medication.[4]

At this time Engel and his associates have trained not only patients with PVCs but also individuals with other forms of cardiac arrhythmias, for example, sinus tachycardia (tachycardia means a faster than normal heart rate), supraventricular tachycardia, paroysmal atrial tachycardia, third degree heart block, atrial fibrillation, and Wolff-Parkinson-White syndrome. The results look very promising and Engel should be recognized as a researcher who has included some of the better follow-up procedures in his studies.

What this research suggests is that not only can people learn to decrease heart rate arrhythmias, but also with proper training and direction they can come to discriminate when their physiological functioning is not working properly and thus avoid or withdraw from situations which produce pathological responses.

7

Raynaud's Disease: Cold Hands or Feet

"Cold hands, warm heart" the old saying goes. Our folklore suggests to us that there is a connection between our physiology and our psychology. It is this very connection that present-day biofeedback researchers are rediscovering and trying to utilize when working with individuals who suffer from cold hands or feet. It is common for some individuals to experience cold hands or feet, especially in certain emotional situations. There are, however, some people who experience cold hands and feet to such an extent that it is painful and the skin turns a bluish color. The formal name for this extreme form of cold hands and feet is Raynaud's disease.

Raynaud's disease is a vascular disorder, first described by Raynaud in the early 1860s. One of the patients that Raynaud originally described was a woman whose fingers would become painful and discolored. This particular woman had taken care of her mother and had been with her mother when the woman died. About a month after the death of the mother the woman began to have painful attacks in her hands and feet, such that they would become cold and blue. The patient would even experience the problem in the middle of examinations by Raynaud. He could find no obvious cause for the attacks.

In the 1930s Mittelmann and Wolff sought to explore the relationship between skin temperature and affective states.[1] These researchers worked with 47 individuals, 5 of whom had been classified as having Raynaud's disease. With all but three of the subjects in the study including those with Raynaud's, there was a decrease in finger temperature during periods of induced emotional stress. The major difference between the Raynaud patients and the others was that the reduction in hand temperature for the Raynaud patients was associated with pain and cyanosis (blueing of the skin). Mittelmann and Wolff suggested that with Raynaud's, the degree of pain and discomfort is associated with both the outside temperature and the degree of emotional stress.

As in hypertension, the origin of Raynaud's disease is unknown although cold and/or emotional factors can trigger the condition in some people. One theory is that during the attack the hands or feet do not receive enough blood for adequate metabolism and the result is a type of pain similar to that experienced around the heart during angina attacks. One treatment of Raynaud's has been surgery, although even with surgery relapses have been reported. Recently, biofeedback researchers have asked if Raynaud's disease could be treated by teaching a person to modify blood flow with the aid of feedback concerning finger temperature. Finger temperature is determined by the amount of blood present in the finger.

This work has been based on basic research both in Russia by Luria and in this country by Snyder and Noble in which it was demonstrated that humans could learn to both increase and decrease blood flow in the fingers.[2] The focus of this early work was to demonstrate that it was possible for an individual to make changes in blood flow which as an autonomic response was considered by many not to be under voluntary control. As you know from the history of biofeedback, it has been demonstrated in a variety of ways that physiological responses including blood flow can be brought under voluntary control.

At this time research utilizing biofeedback with such disorders as Raynaud's disease is just beginning. We, of course, cannot know if biofeedback will become a treatment of choice but the results look promising. For example, the following is a successful case study reported in a recent review of biofeedback by David Shapiro and Richard Surwit.[3]

> The first of these cases involves a patient treated for over a year at the Allen Memorial Institute of McGill University. Upon referral, the

patient, a 21-year-old female, had been suffering from Raynaud's disease for about five years and had both cervical and lumbar sympathectomies. Training consisted of a temperature feedback procedure. A sensitive termistor was mounted on the patient's left hand. If there was a net increase in temperature in excess of 0.1° C, the patient was given feedback. This consisted of a bell, a flashing light, and an increment in a cumulative graph displayed on a videoscope. The therapist would then verbally reinforce the patient for her success. Each session consisted of three 10-minute trials separated by five or ten minute rest periods. Fourteen sessions were administered over a three-week period after which time the patient stopped treatment for one month to go on vacation. Upon her return, sessions were administered twice a week and consisted of two ten-minute trials for each hand. This mode of therapy lasted for four months and was supplemented by counseling and assertive training (Wolpe, 1958) for family problems. All therapy was then discontinued for one month and then feedback training was resumed at weekly intervals for the next six months. Since the beginning of training, this patient managed to increase her basal hand temperature (both hands) from an average of 23° C to 26.6° C. She no longer required elaborate protective garments for the winter and markedly decreased the number of Raynaud's attacks she experienced.

Edward Taub at the Institute for Behavioral Research in Maryland has performed some pilot work with five patients suffering from Raynaud's.[4] At times, these patients' hand temperature demonstrated little blood flow. Biofeedback training sessions were begun in which the patients learned to increase whole hand temperature. In general, their hand temperature increased to the normal range with training. One woman was able to increase her hand temperature by the phenomenal amount of 17.75° F.

These are remarkable results for a laboratory, but what about the real world in which cold weather and/or stress can bring on an attack of Raynaud's? In order to simulate a sudden change in temperature, Edward Taub and his associates designed a suit in which the inside part was composed of small tubing through which water could be pushed quickly. Imagine that you are now in such a suit and 60° water suddenly comes through the suit. What happens? If you only sit there, your hand temperature will drop 5° to 8° F. according to Dr. Taub. However, Dr. Taub was able to teach one Raynaud patient to prevent that drop through biofeedback training and in fact this patient was even able to increase her hand temperature by almost 2° F. while 60° water was in the suit for 10 minutes. It is amazing that just a few years ago a description of Dr. Taub's experiment would have been received with about the same level of belief as a description of Tibetan monks sitting in icy streams doing Dumo breathing and not dying of the cold. Are there other effects of biofeedback training with Raynaud's patients? Eric Peper suggests that the answer to this question is yes.

Dr. Peper emphasizes the importance of the overall changes that accompany biofeedback training.[5] He uses the word "trainee" for an individual just beginning to learn a new skill or process, in this case biofeedback.

> For example, with trainees who suffer from chronic peripheral cold, such as found in Raynaud's disease, we have noted feelings of helplessness and shrinking away from the world. The person literally stops expanding his energy and shrinks. When the person stops shrinking by accepting where he "is," or feeling the energy expanding, the hands warm up.
>
> Thermal feedback is a tool whereby a trainee learns to change peripheral warmth and was used with one trainee who had Raynaud's disease. As shown in Figure 2 she changed her attitude while attempting to warm her hands, from active to passive volition. As she grew from nonacceptance to self-acceptance, her temperature increased markedly between the 7th and 10th minute. Once her attitude changed, she experienced an insight of how her attitude created her physical symptoms. By withdrawing her psychological and emotional energy from the people around her, she created the physical symptoms of chronic, peripheral coldness. As the physiological system is alleviated, the underlying psychological difficulty frequently emerges in a striking demonstration of the interaction between mind and body. By attempting to control her autonomic system through biofeedback learning, she had to contact her conscious and unconscious processes and reestablish a harmonious state between mind and body.

From these case studies, two points are clear to us. The first is that one cannot ignore the emotional factors when treating a disorder that has as important psychosomatic aspects as does Raynaud's disease. That is, you must realize that biofeedback is not just a mechanical technique which puts to sleep attitudes, feelings, and thoughts while the training procedure is going on. The second point is that it is unknown if biofeedback itself is the

FIGURE 2

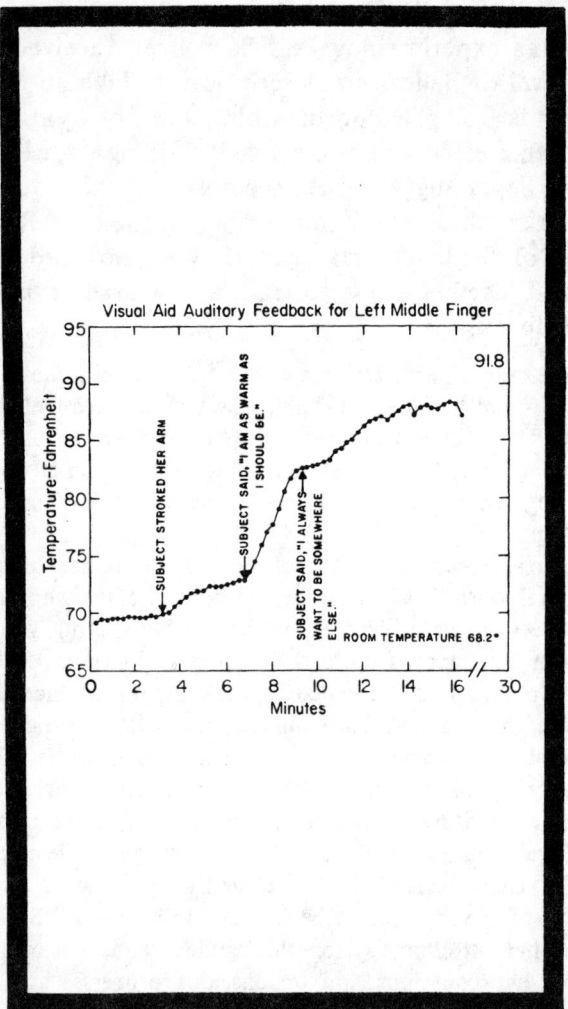

Source: E. Peper. Case study presented at the annual meeting of the American Psychological Association, 1974.

most important aspect of the training. The research and treatment of Raynaud's is in such an early stage that it is impossible to know which factors are most important in the treatment, although it does appear that biofeedback will prove to be a useful procedure.

8
Asthma

Take a deep breath. As you took a breath, your chest became enlarged by the action of your muscles. Your diaphragm and even your ribs moved in order to increase the size of your chest. Air came in through your nose and continued toward your lungs through a tube called the trachea. The trachea divides into two main branches called bronchi and these in turn into smaller passages called bronchioles which make up part of your lungs. Now relax and let the air out. As you can see the expiration of air is basically a passive movement in which the chest works like a bellows to force air out of the lungs. With asthma, the normal passive movement of the air is restricted and it is particularly difficult to breathe out. What normally happens in people without asthma is that the natural elastic tension of the lung tissue tends to keep the bronchi open. However, in asthma the smaller bronchi and the bronchioles are narrowed by a spasm of the muscles and the swelling of their walls. This resistance may cause the asthmatic to begin an inhalation before he or she has finished breathing out. Thus, air becomes trapped in the chest. This produces the wheezing sensation that asthmatics experience during an attack. The most common form of treatment for asthma at this time is to inhale a medication that will open the bronchioles and allow the person to breathe normally.[1]

Asthma is a problem that has only recently been approached with a biofeedback technology. Thus in this chapter we will report what little work has been performed and discuss some of the psychological factors associated with asthma. One of the main difficulties of applying biofeedback to the asthmatic condition is that of finding a suitable measure upon which feedback can be given. It is of course impossible to watch or record changes from the bronchi themselves, yet their role in the increased airway resistance is without dispute. Some researchers have attempted to measure airway resistance itself, but this requires that the patient breathe into a large tube which is somewhat unnatural and uncomfortable. Thus, measures of breathing related to asthma are difficult to take but nevertheless there have been a few attempts to modify asthmatic responses with guarded but positive results.

Before discussing the utilization of biofeedback with asthma, let us examine some of the psychological factors related to asthma. One of the early psychological theories connected with asthma was that of Alexander. He suggested that asthma is related to an unresolved dependency of a person on his or her mother. What the asthma attack represents according to Alexander is a suppressed cry for the mother when there is a threat of her separation from the child.

It is difficult for some people to accept this type of psychological reasoning as presented by Alexander since it is largely based on case reports and lacks systematic observation. Yet, in clinical experience (not with biofeedback), we have seen people who fit the description of Alexander perfectly.[2] In one particular case, the person was asked to imagine he was a child again and to describe what was going on in his life. He closed his eyes and remembered himself in a crib. Then he began to describe his mother leaving the room and that he wanted attention. Right at the moment in which it looked as if he was going to get angry, he had what appeared to be a mild asthma attack. Whether one can say that dependency is the "cause" of asthma or not is, of course, an open question. However, there is little doubt that asthma attacks can be brought on by psychological factors.[3]

A study that demonstrates the importance of psychological factors was one in which both asthmatics and normal subjects were led to believe that they were inhaling a substance which would cause constriction of the bronchi. In actuality, the substance was only a solution which contained salt. During the experiment, the subjects without asthma showed no reaction to the solution whereas almost half of the asthmatics showed a reaction and their bronchi did indeed constrict. Other researchers have followed asthmatics throughout psychotherapy sessions and found that over 90 percent of the attacks were preceded by psychological stimuli. The evidence strongly suggests that psychological factors are important in gaining a complete understanding of asthma.[4]

Relatively few biofeedback studies have been performed with asthmatics because it is difficult to give exact feedback and the procedure requires expensive respiratory and computing equipment. Still, there have been a few attempts to utilize biofeedback. At this point the measure of airway resistance seems to be the most important measure and it is possible to give continuous feedback of it. One study that utilized this measure was performed by Levenson, Manuck, Strupp, Blackwood, and Snell and reported at the convention of the Biofeedback Research Society in 1974.[5] In this study, respiratory resistance was measured on each breath and with the aid of a digital computer, feedback was given to the subjects on a breath-by-breath basis. Although these researchers reported some success, they themselves question the real clinical value of the technique since the actual changes overall were small and not long lasting. Another study reported in 1976 was performed by Vachon and Rich.[6] In this study mild asthmatics were trained to decrease total respiratory resistance through the use of visual feedback. As in the case of some of the early heart rate control studies, the subjects in this study were not told what response they were to change, only that they were to keep the green light on. In this case, the green light represented decreases in total airway resistance. The results of the study do tend to suggest that mild asthmatics given feedback can learn to decrease total respiratory resistance. However, Vachon and Rich point out that the level of decrease with biofeedback was no more than that experienced with one inhalation of a common asthma medication. Dr. Feldman also utilized total respiratory resistance in a study in which he worked with four children who suffered from asthma.[7] In this study he sought to decrease total respiratory resistance and reported that the children could learn to decrease their airway resistance even after short sessions of biofeedback. However, although Feldman is positive on the potential for biofeedback as a treatment for asthma, he does point out that asthmatics may require some type of "maintenance" treatment sessions of biofeedback to continue the lowered airway resistance.

Since the problems of biofeedback-assisted changes in respiratory resistance seem large as compared to the magnitude of changes produced, we must ask, are there other nondrug alternatives? The answer is yes. In research it has been demonstrated that not only painful memories from childhood produce a restriction of respiratory output but that relaxation will facilitate normal breathing in asthmatics.[8] From this finding, research has been started in which asthmatics are taught to relax as a means of preventing asthmatic attacks. In one case study there was a drastic reduction in the need for medication after only a two week period of relaxation training and this continued for the follow-up period of two months.[9] How about relaxation with biofeedback? Relaxation training aided by biofeedback is also being utilized to treat asthma and the results appear promising.[10] In these studies, individuals with asthma are taught to relax through biofeedback procedures. More about the procedures themselves later. The initial results do suggest that biofeedback relaxation techniques are superior to just relaxation itself.

Of course there are a number of factors such as severity of the asthma, the degree to which it is an allergic reaction, the patient's feeling toward taking medication, and even his or her feeling about asthma itself that enter into the successful utilization of any treatment, either drug or nondrug. Biofeedback is no exception. For those who do not wish to continue medicinal treatments and thus have the motivation for training either with the reduction of respiratory resistance or relaxation, then the promise is greatly improved. For the general population, it appears as if it will be some time, if ever, before biofeedback can be considered a major treatment for asthma.

9

Epilepsy

For at least the past 2,000 years, epilepsy has been seen as being more than just a disorder. It has been thought to be a visitation from the gods by some, and this is reflected in the name "sacred disease." Although Hippocrates suggested that epilepsy was no more a visitation of the gods than any other disease, we still find epilepsy playing an important role in medicine and literature. Hughlings Jackson who is credited with ushering in the modern era in clinical neurology, suggested that our understanding of the "dreamy states" of epilepsy would be the key to the understanding of insanity. Dostoyevsky wrote in "The Idiot" the following description of an epileptic attack.

> The air was filled with a big noise and I thought it had engulfed me. I have really touched God. He came into me myself. Yes God exists, I cried, and I don't remember anything else. You all, healthy people, he said, can't imagine the happiness which we epileptics feel during the second before our fit. Mahomet, in his Koran, said he had seen paradise and had gone into it. All these stupid clever men are quite sure he was a liar and a charlatan. But no, he did not lie. He really had been in paradise during an attack of epilepsy; he was a victim of this disease like I was. I don't know if this felicity lasts for seconds, hours, or months, but believe me, for all the joys that life may bring, I would not exchange this one (Dostoyevsky, 1868).

What do we know of this disorder that has had among its sufferers such men as Julius Caesar, Napoleon, Van Gogh and

Dostoyevsky? Surprisingly little. One prominent medical textbook suggests that a satisfactory definition of epilepsy on the basis of clinical characteristics is nonexistent. About the best we can do is to discuss the seizure, and even here about all we can do is to classify different types of seizures. We say that the common characteristic is a spontaneous and massive discharge of neurons. Associated with the discharge may be changes in thought or behavioral processes. These may include the person falling to the ground and losing consciousness as epilepsy is often portrayed in literature. The most common treatment for epilepsy is a form of anticonvulsant medication. However, recently biofeedback is being explored as a form of treatment.

In Washington and elsewhere around the country, senators and others often ask why a scientist should really care what the brain wave pattern of a cat looks like and, more, why should government money be used to finance such studies. Scientists often find themselves in a difficult position because they themselves can't give an answer, or at best the scientist must reply that the question seems as if it is an important one to them—hardly the answer the normal taxpayer wants to hear come April 15. Yet at times discoveries are made which lead in new directions because someone is doing good basic research. The development of biofeedback treatments of epilepsy has such a history.

Let us look at a cat and the electrical activity of his brain. Dr. Sterman and his associates at UCLA and the Sepulveda V.A. Hospital were interested in the brain wave patterns or EEG of motionless cats.

Of particular interest to them was a characteristic 12-14 Hz. brain wave rhythm that appeared when the cat was still. This brain wave activity is called sensorimotor rhythm (SMR). Dr. Sterman demonstrated that a cat could be rewarded for producing this rhythm in a manner similar to the way a rat is conditioned to press a bar in a Skinner box.[1]

In a Skinner box, an animal is given food or other desired substances each time that it performs the appropriate behavior. The most common example is to give a rat food for pressing a bar. In Dr. Sterman's research, the cat was rewarded with either food or positive brain stimulation whenever SMR activity was present. Cats conditioned in this manner would assume a motionless posture and experience prolonged periods of sustained sleep in which there was an enhancement of a certain type of EEG activity called spindle burst activity. However, what was to be of most importance for the application of biofeedback to epilepsy was the finding that these cats showed a resistance to seizures which had been experimentally induced by drugs. This finding led Sterman and his colleagues to search for a human analogue. Indeed, they found what they believe to be a SMR-like rhythm in man. The question was how could a person, particularly an epileptic, be taught to increase the occurrence of this rhythm and what would be the outcome?

Dr. Sterman and his colleague, Dr. Friar, worked with a 23-year-old woman who had been experiencing seizures irregularly at a rate of about two per month.[2] The woman was seated in a dimly lit room and told to keep her eyes open and to relax her mind. Placed in front and above her was a feedback unit which contained two rows of colored lights. The lights would come on to represent the presence of the SMR-like rhythm in the woman and in this manner she received feedback concerning her brain wave pattern. The results were striking and we will use the authors' own words.

> Concurrent with evidence for acquisition of the SMR response by the third session, there were no further seizures for a period of three months. Additionally, the patient showed some interesting changes in personality during the course of training. Having previously been a quiet and unobtrusive individual, she progressively became more outgoing, showing increased personal confidence and an enhanced interest in her appearance. She also spontaneously reported experiencing a shorter latency to sleep onset, a more restful sleep, as indicated by a reduction of her normal physical reorientation in bed throughout a night, and a more rapid awakening in the morning. None of the latter changes could be documented objectively, but they were particularly interesting in terms of the similar, quantified findings obtained with SMR in the cat.

With the successful treatment of one case for a short period of time, the question remained as to whether biofeedback could become a useful treatment. Two other laboratories began to test this possibility. One lab was that of Joel Lubar at the University of Tennessee and the other was that of William Finley at the Children's Medical Center in Tulsa. Dr. Finley and his associates worked with a 13-year-old boy who had a history of convulsions dating back to age 2.[3] These authors report that their patient was averaging 75 seizures per ten hours of wakefulness. These seizures were of such a type that the boy would fall to the ground with the loss of consciousness and muscle tone. The training was similar to that used by Sterman consisting of a light and tone serving as feedback to the boy. The researchers also introduced a game-like quality to the training in which the child would be given a certain amount of money if he could produce the SMR-like brain wave pattern enough times before a clock in front of him stopped. Most researchers report that biofeedback lends itself to games and this allows for the necessary motivation to keep children interested in the task at hand. During and after a period of training that lasted from July to the following January, the child showed a striking reduction of seizures. By the end of the study, the boy was not totally seizure free, yet the percent of seizures in which he did not fall to the ground had increased and his total seizure rate was decreasing.

In the first of two reports, Lubar and his associates attempted to replicate what Sterman had found with his one patient and what Finley had found with his one patient.[4] Lubar chose to treat six patients—three males and three females—who ranged in age from 12 to 19 years. He used a similar type of feedback in which a light denoted the presence of the SMR-like brain pattern, and reported that of the six patients, five showed significant reductions in seizure rate during the first three to four months of training. In the second report, he extended the original training to cover a period of nine months to a year and also added two new patients.[5] The newer report also confirms that the majority of patients not only show a reduction in seizures but that also the seizures are of shorter duration and less intense than initially.

Although there are still many unanswered questions as to why biofeedback works with epileptics, and whether the effects will be long lasting, there is room for optimism. Lubar concludes his report by pointing to future directions.

> The greatest advantage of the biofeedback approach for the management of epileptic seizures is that it offers a hope for the severe epileptic

whose medication is not sufficient and whose seizures are extremely debilitating. At the present time only 75 percent of all epileptics maintained on anticonvulsant therapy are adequately managed by such therapy. The research of our laboratory, and others using SMR conditioning, is now directed toward the refractory epileptic. Perhaps this method might be even more potent for epileptics whose seizures can be maintained by drugs, but where it would be desirable to use voluntary control rather than rely on drugs which have severe and debilitating side effects. It is important to realize that epilepsy is associated with strong psychological dependencies and a marked tendency by patients to seek secondary gain from their condition. The ability of patients, through voluntary control, to modulate their own brain waves and their own seizures—first with the use of biofeedback equipment, and later without—should be most gratifying and self-reinforcing. This in itself might help to reduce dependency and provide the epileptic an opportunity for building self-confidence.

It should be added that the biofeedback work with epilepsy is only in the exploratory stages. It requires a high degree of sophistication both in terms of equipment and in terms of electrophysiological interpretations to perform these studies. This suggests that it may be some time before it is commonly utilized. Also, whether biofeedback of the sensorimotor rhythm is really the active ingredient which leads to a lessening of epileptic seizures is a topic presently being investigated.[6] However, it must be noted that the patients who were treated by biofeedback were in some cases those who did not respond to medication and were given biofeedback training only as a last resort. This suggests that biofeedback should be seen as achieving success when traditional treatments failed. As a whole, the techniques appear promising for making epilepsy not a sacred disorder as was once thought but a secular problem that can be dealt with by the generalized procedures of biofeedback.

10

Tension Headaches

Judging from the medication ads that we see on television one would think that headaches were the one common characteristic shared by all of us humans. Of course this is not the case, yet the headache remains a common problem that receives relatively little attention in the medical and psychological literature despite its interest to the pharmaceutical industry. In one recent review of the psychological studies dealing with headaches, it was suggested that, paradoxically, the medical community considers headaches to be a psychological problem whereas the psychological community considers headaches to be a physiological problem.[1] This may result from the fact that headaches for most individuals will cease to be a problem after *either* a short rest or a mild form of medication, usually one that contains salicylic acid such as aspirin.

Although headaches have been classified into some 15 different categories, the two which will be of interest to us are those of tension or muscle contraction headaches and those of migraine. The former will be discussed here and the latter in the next chapter. It is generally believed that muscle contraction or tension headaches are the result of sustained contraction (tension) of skeletal muscles around the face, particularly the back of the neck and the forehead. There has been strong suggestion that this tension may be brought on by psychological factors. Dr. Malmo and his associates have been studying the relationship of psychological and physiological variables since the 1940s.[2] One common meas-

ure of muscle tension that is utilized in their research is the electromyogram or EMG as it is usually called. As we discussed earlier, the EMG is a record of the electrical activity that is given off by the muscles from which we are recording. In general, high amplitude EMG records represent muscle activity and tension whereas low amplitude ones represent resting or relaxed states. In one case study described by Dr. Malmo, a 28-year-old woman complained of a tightness on the right side of her neck. This particular woman was not married and she feared contact with men. The woman's psychological history was seen to play an important role in her present problem since her mother had severely punished her as a child for what the mother believed was sex play with the woman's brother. At the time the woman was seen in Dr. Malmo's clinic, she said that she had considered marriage but only on the condition that there would be no sexual intercourse.

During the period in which EMG recordings were made from this woman in Dr. Malmo's laboratory the psychological aspects of her muscle tension became very plain. Once while the woman was just resting, EMG was being taken from the neck and arm. Then a male assistant began to remove the electrodes from her arm and while he was doing this he moved her arm by taking her hand in his. With this contact by a man even though casual, the EMG activity from the right side of her neck increased—showing tension—while the EMG from the left side did not change. The change in tension was also shown during an interview. The discussion of certain psychological material increased the EMG level in her neck to 10-20 times that of her arm. Although it is clear from this case study that muscle tension may be produced by psychological factors, the next question to be asked is whether individuals can be trained to reduce muscle tension and if this training would be helpful for coping with tension headaches.

One of the earliest research groups to test this idea with biofeedback was that of Tom Budzynski, Johann Stoyva, and Charles Adler.[3] These researchers first had to decide from which muscle group they should give feedback. They decided that since tension headaches are the result of a tightening of the neck and scalp muscles, that the muscles on the forehead (frontalis muscle) might give a good indication of tension levels.

The procedure in this study was as follows. The person would come to the laboratory and during the first two sessions, he or she would be asked just to relax. During these two sessions no biofeedback would be given the person but the researchers did make recordings of the EMG levels. After the initial visits to the laboratory, the person would then be given feedback which was proportional to the degree of muscle tension which was present. That is, if the frontalis muscles were very tense, the individual would hear a high pitched tone; whereas if the muscles were relaxed, the tone would be low pitched. In this manner the person could tell instantaneously when the muscle tension in his or her forehead became greater or lessened. The person was instructed to keep the tone in the low pitched range as this represented a relaxed state.

Did the training procedure work? To answer this question, Budzynski, Stoyva and Adler needed to ask two questions. First, did the person show reductions in the amount of muscle tension during the month or two of the training? That is, did the biofeedback procedure work? The second question is the more important one when considering clinical applications of biofeedback. Did the person experience fewer headaches? Remember, the study began by assuming that there was a connection between muscle tension and headaches and then sought to determine if reducing muscle tension would also reduce the number of headaches that a person experienced. The answer to both questions was yes. Both muscle tension and number of reported headaches decreased over the training period. Also, an interview with the persons involved in the study revealed that headache levels were still low, five months after the biofeedback training.

Great results, you might say. However, the history of medical and psychological treatments is overflowing with reports of successful cures following the introduction of a new technique whether it be medication or meditation. This is not to say that the people who claim to be cured are lying, for in actuality they have improved medically. What you have to realize is that it may not have been the treatment itself, but the expectation of the treatment that produced the change for the better.

In order to better determine the role of biofeedback in the muscle relaxation therapy that was used by Drs. Budzynski, Stoyva and Adler, these same researchers along with Daniel Mullaney set out to perform a control study similar to their previous one.[4] In the new study the researchers reasoned that if a group were treated in the same way as the original biofeedback group but not given real feedback concerning their muscle tension, then the difference between the two groups should reflect the effect of the biofeedback. Thus, in the new study a group of subjects received feedback which was related to muscle activity of the frontalis muscle and a second group, a control group, did not receive feedback in terms of their muscle activity. What if in the first study relaxation came from just hearing the tone from the feedback go up and down? In order to control for this possibility in the second study these researchers played a tape recording of the tone that was present in the real biofeedback condition. That is, the second group received feedback but the feedback was not related to muscle activity. Thus, the feedback that they were hearing had nothing to do with their own physiological functioning, and served as a control for just hearing a tone. As an added control, these researchers had a third group of headache sufferers who were asked just to keep a chart of the number of headaches that they had during a two month period, and that they would receive biofeedback training at the end of the two months, which they did. This third group would help to determine if there were suggestibility factors associated with just signing up for the treatment and if headaches would go away with no treatment at all.

It may seem strange to you that headache sufferers would report improvement without any treatment at all. Yet, study after study has demonstrated that just coming to a clinic without receiving any treatment often results in improvement of whatever the problem was. Stranger yet, just calling on the phone and setting up an appointment may also result in an improvement of the problem. The doctor is almost always right when he follows any prescription with the words "it should be better by morning." Almost everything is. The general term for this phenomenon is the placebo effect.[5] It is of course not a new phenomenon, for 2,000 years ago it was written, "No prophet is acceptable in his village, no physician heals those who know him."[6] Neither is this phenomenon limited to the healing profession, for in the 1920s a series of studies was carried out to determine optimal working conditions.[7] In these studies a group of women who assembled telephone equipment were placed in different working conditions in which length of working day, number of rest periods, and other factors in their environment were systematically changed. The effects of the study were surprising. The experimenters found that with each major change in working conditions, the level of output increased. The women were then returned to their original working conditions and to everyone's surprise, output again increased and to a level higher than it had been during any of the experimental conditions. How could this be explained? Working conditions were as they had always been. What was different, of course, was that these women had been made special and given attention. This alone was enough to change the level of output. The location where the studies were conducted has lent its name to this phenomenon (the Hawthorne effect) which every researcher who works with people has either to learn or to repeat the rest of his or her experimental life.

But back to biofeedback. Not only did the biofeedback group demonstrate a greater ability to decrease muscle tension over the period of the study, but also in this group the number of headaches was reduced more than in the other groups. These findings suggest that biofeedback was a useful treatment for tension headaches. However, to determine if there were any lasting effects, the researchers contacted the headache sufferers a year and a half later. Of those contacted the majority reported that their headaches had remained at a low level. We feel that this is a very important study for two reasons. First, it showed that biofeedback can be a useful treatment for tension headache and second, it is one of the few studies that has included a long term follow-up to determine if biofeedback training has a lasting effect.

It may be that the real use of biofeedback in this area will be to teach headache sufferers how to recognize that they are beginning to tense their neck muscles and thus begin a relaxing procedure wherever they are. Here you are sitting in another one of those meetings that you hate and all of a sudden you realize, "I am getting tense." What do you do? Well, you could either do what you always do which is to keep getting tighter until the meeting is over and you have a headache, or you could begin to relax in the manner that you may have previously learned through biofeedback training. It is apparent that if biofeedback is to work, it will not be biofeedback alone, but a combination of biofeedback training and the person's willingness to hear the feedback from his or her own body. Next time you are in a place you don't want to be, think about your alternatives to having a headache. The choice is yours.

11
Migraine Headaches

Migraine headaches are said to have affected Caesar, St. Paul, Kant, and Freud. It is a disorder that has been classified and written about for at least two thousand years. Today, it is estimated that 5 to 15 percent of the general population suffer from migraine attacks. What is a migraine headache and what causes it? Taking the last question first, we have to report that the cause of migraines is unknown. Although we know that there are biochemical changes in migraines (as in almost everything else from sleep to eating), the specific factors remain unknown. Two thousand years ago, it was believed that too much yellow or black bile in the body was the cause of migraines. Later attempts were made to alleviate these headaches with such cures as blood-letting in the 16th century, or more recently with liver pills. Presently, some forms of medication have proven to be helpful to some migraine sufferers. Others have tried almost every drug without much success.

Turning to the question of defining migraine headaches, we may note that at least over the last 100 years the descriptions have remained similar. In 1860, du Bois Reymond, the famous neurophysiologist, wrote the following description of the migraine.

> Since about my twentieth year, though otherwise in good health, I have suffered from migraine. Every three or four weeks I am liable to an attack ... I wake with a general feeling of disorder, and a slight pain in the region of the right temple which, without overstepping the

midline, reaches its greatest intensity at midday; towards evening it usually passes off. While at rest the pain is bearable, but it is increased by motion to a high degree of violence.... It responds to each beat of the temporal artery. The latter feels, on the affected side, like a hard cord, while the left is in its normal condition. The countenance is pale and sunken, the right eye small and reddened. At the height of the attack, when it is a violent one, there is nausea.... There may be left behind a slight gastric disorder; frequently, also, the scalp remains tender at one spot the following morning.... For a certain period after the attack I can expose myself with impunity to influences which before would have infallibly caused an attack.[1]

More recently a classification was proposed for migraine headaches in the *Journal of the American Medical Association*. It reads as follows:

Recurrent attacks of headache, widely varied in intensity, frequency, and duration. The attacks are commonly unilateral in onset; are usually associated with anorexia and, sometimes, with nausea and vomiting; in some are preceded by, or associated with, conspicuous sensory, motor, and mood disturbance, and are often familial.[2]

Biofeedback first became applied to migraine headaches in a serendipitous manner. Drs. Sargent, Green and Walters at the Menninger Clinic observed the hands of a woman in their laboratory as she was recovering from a migraine attack.[3] Her hands became flushed and within two minutes there was an increase of 10 degrees Fahrenheit in her hand temperature. This suggested to them that training in hand temperature control might be a method of decreasing the incidence of migraine attacks. They performed an initial study in which 15 migraine patients were given feedback training in controlling hand temperature. In addition, the subjects in this study were taught autogenic training phrases such as "my hands feel heavy" and "my hands are warm." After a period of a few months in which the headache sufferers were trained both in the laboratory and at home with a portable biofeedback unit, these researchers reported that 12 of the 15 patients were evaluated as improved.

Eric Peper and Elmer Grossman decided to utilize the biofeedback-autogenic technique described above with two children who suffered from migraines.[4] The first child was nine years of age.

She had suffered from vertigo and vomiting beginning at the age of three. From then until her present age of nine the vertigo lessened and attacks of migraines became more regular. The second girl who was 13 had also experienced vomiting and severe headaches from an early age. Both girls were taught to increase their hand temperature through biofeedback, and could increase it as much as 8 to 10 degrees F. In addition, these children learned autogenic-like phrases which represented an increase in temperature (images such as warm toast, lobsters, ovens, summer) and in their ability to gain control over themselves. An interesting finding of this report was that not only did the training prove successful but also that it occurred very quickly for these children. These authors suggest that part of the quickness of the autogenic-biofeedback technique may have been because these individuals were children and had not yet learned that they could not control their own physiology. A more recent report by Diamond and Franklin with a larger number of children also found that a combination of autogenic training and biofeedback demonstrated good results in the majority of cases.[5]

Just recently, a new approach for the treatment of migraine has been proposed. This approach is also a biofeedback approach but rather than working on raising the temperature of the hand as had been done previously, this approach emphasized changing the level of blood flow to an artery in the scalp. The reasoning for this approach is as follows. One characteristic of what is called classical migraine is that there is a period before the headache in which the blood vessels of the head constrict. Following the initial constriction, there is an abnormally great enlargement of the blood vessels. The result of this drastic change is the migraine headache. It is further suggested that the pain of the migraine headache is caused by an increased pressure from the enlarged blood vessels which in turn causes contact with sensitive pain fibers. The treatment for migraine pain is often a medication such as ergotamine tartrate which produces a constriction of the blood vessels. Since other procedures beside medication, for example placing pressure on the carotid artery may offer temporary relief, it has been reasoned that if a person were taught through biofeedback to constrict one particular artery in the scalp, then this would bring relief.

One of the first published studies to test this hypothesis was that of Linda Friar and Jackson Beatty.[6] These researchers found 19 people who had migraine headaches. The idea was to teach these individuals through the use of biofeedback to decrease pulse amplitude in the temporal artery. Since the study sought to examine a specific biofeedback technique for the treatment of migraine, it was necessary to have a control group that was treated similarly in every way except that this group would not receive feedback from the temporal artery. These researchers decided that pulse volume feedback from the hand would serve as a good control. The results of this study are impressive. Whereas there was a significant reduction of major migraine headaches for the group given biofeedback training of the temporal artery, the group receiving feedback from the hand (the control group) showed no major reduction of migraine attacks.

There are a number of questions that researchers must ask. If you are a migraine sufferer, your only question is, "Does it work?" The evidence seems to show that a combination of autogenic training and biofeedback does something that in turn decreases the frequency of migraine attacks. At this point in time there are only a few studies that have attempted to determine whether biofeedback is necessary, whether autogenic training is necessary or whether it is a combination of biofeedback and autogenic training that is necessary. Of course, in the final analysis it may turn out that just relaxation, that certain types of images, or that the process of imagining is the active ingredient in the alleviation of migraine headaches. Until that time, we will have to wait.

12

Stomach and Intestinal Disorders

We recently gave a questionnaire to hundreds of college students in which we asked them what bodily change they notice in themselves in a real-life stress situation.[1] The results indicated that "nervous stomach," which some described as vague abdominal pain and others even as diarrhea, was the most frequently noted bodily change during stress. We realize that bodily change during stress varies somewhat from person to person, with the majority of people being stomach responders while others are heart rate responders or sweaters or the like. Two processes take place in the gastrointestinal (g.i.) system and malfunction of either or both can cause the discomfort that we label as "nervous stomach."[2]

The first process is motility. The muscles of the stomach and intestines contract and relax much like the heart. The function of this is to mix and propel forward the contents. The stomach contracts approximately three times a minute and the intestines slightly faster. The second process is secretion. Acid and other chemicals are released for the purpose of breaking down and digesting the food you have eaten.

What is commonly referred to as a stomach ache is often really an intestinal ache. Your stomach is approximately the size of your closed fist and is situated about an inch to the left of your navel and up a couple of inches extending under your ribs. Your intestines are much larger, filling most of the remainder of your abdomen. In France, most distress emanating from the abdomen is thought of as originating in the liver.[3]

MOTILITY

Returning to the motility or rate of contraction of the stomach and intestines, how can biofeedback be used to slow it down or speed it up? The primary stumbling block here is obtaining a measure of this internal bodily response. This problem of how to record stomach and intestinal motility without causing discomfort to the patient and without interfering with normal g.i. activity still has not been completely resolved and is the reason why there has been so little progress in this area.

How Gastrointestinal Motility Is Recorded

The most commonly-used method of recording g.i. motility is to have the patient swallow a balloon, or condum, deflated of course, attached to a flexible tube. After the balloon is in place, (inexperienced subjects usually gag and regurgitate it a couple of times) it is inflated so that it fills the stomach. The end of the tube not attached to the balloon is connected to a device that measures pressure. As the patient's stomach contracts, the pressure in the balloon increases and this increase in pressure is recorded. What's wrong with this method other than the fact that you have to swallow a balloon and throw-up a couple of times? The technical shortcoming is that the balloon stimulates the inside of the stomach causing it to contract, thereby interfering with the measure being recorded.[4]

A more recently developed method for recording g.i. motility involves the use of a miniature pressure-sensitive device, a miniature transmitter and miniature batteries. All of this is packaged in pill form, about the size of a horse pill, and is swallowed by the human subject. A receiver is placed next to the patient which picks up the signal being transmitted from the pill, the frequency of which changes as a function of the pressure wherever the pill is. The "wherever" part turned out to be a problem since g.i. motility changes from one part of the g.i. system to the next and there was no way to know where the pill was. But medical technology cannot be stumped that easily. The manufacturer of the pill suggested that users of it tie a string around it, with the string being the correct length so that the pill would remain in the desired portion of the g.i. system. The other end of the pill was to be tied, you guessed it, to the patient's tooth. On the one hand, the string method proved impractical because the subjects gagged a lot which interfered with normal g.i. activity. On the other hand, the string method made retrieval of the pill a lot easier. Each pill costs approximately $25 and was made to be retrieved, sterilized, and reused. Prior to the advent of the string method the investigator had to depend upon the subject finding the pill and returning it to the laboratory or clinic. The pill was then sterilized and it was hoped that the next subject would not find out where it had been.

Surface Methods of Recording

One method that we think shows a great deal of promise involves placing electrodes on the skin over the stomach or intestine and recording g.i. activity in much the same way that an electrocardiogram is recorded with electrodes on your chest. This surface recording technique which was developed by R. C. Davis and his associates[5] is simple to use, painless to the patient and in no way interferes with normal ongoing g.i. activity.

Deckner, Hill and Bourne[6] used this surface recording technique in conjunction with biofeedback to train normal subjects to increase and decrease the frequency of their stomach contractions. The subjects were trained in five sessions, each consisting of 24 minutes of biofeedback in the form of visual inspection of their record and an auditory signal which corresponded to their stomach activity. The authors reported that three of their four subjects learned to control their stomach activity and concluded that "gastric motility may be a relatively easy response to control."

Milton Harris[7] conducted a study in our laboratory similar to the above except he compared the ability of individuals who suffered from g.i. distress and those who suffered from migraine headaches to control their stomach activity and hand temperature. (See chapter on migraine headaches for a discussion of the relationship of hand temperature to migraine headaches.) Dr. Harris hypothesized that people with g.i. distress would have relatively less difficulty controlling their hand temperature and more difficulty controlling their stomach activity than those who suffered migraines. His results basically supported this hypothesis.

Dr. S. Furmen[8] turned to another technique of providing biofeedback of g.i. activity in order to help five patients who suffered from a lifetime of diarrhea so severe that they were virtually toiletbound. Furmen used the amplified sound from a stethoscope placed on the patient's skin over the intestine to provide feedback of the internal activity. The patients were requested alternately to increase and decrease their g.i. activity while listening to the amplified intestinal sounds. When the sounds increased or decreased appropriately Furmen praised the patient.

After five training sessions all of the patients showed some degree of control over their intestinal sounds. And, more importantly, when questioned about their diarrhea, all had experienced an improvement in their condition. Details of one case successfully treated by Furmen follow.

S. J. is a 24-year-old married woman who before biofeedback treatment suffered from abdominal cramps and diarrhea as frequently as 15 times per day. She had been hospitalized twice and no organic cause for her condition could be found. Standard drugs for diarrhea only reduced the intensity of her symptoms. At her best she experienced four to five loose bowel movements a day. In biofeedback training sessions, S. J. quickly learned to control her intestinal sounds. After three weekly sessions she was able to turn it off and on at will. And her symptoms also quickly decreased. In the six-month period from the end of the biofeedback training until Furmen reported this case she had only three mild attacks. During the latter three months of this period she was completely symptom free! According to Furmen, "For the first time, she has taken a job with confidence and enthusiasm."

Fecal Incontinence

The next g.i. disorder which has been treated successfully by biofeedback to which we will turn our attention is fecal incontinence. Individuals who suffer from fecal incontinence usually have normal bowel movements but are unable to control *when* they defecate. Their difficulty is not in their stomach or intestine but rather in a small circle of muscle called the external rectal sphincter. This is what opens and closes, controlling when feces leave the rectum. In normal individuals, an increase in rectal pressure caused by the presence of feces, automatically causes contraction of the external sphincter. This is referred to as the rectosphincteric reflex.

In the first phase of a pioneering investigation, Engel, Nikoomanash and Schuster[9] checked the degree of impairment of the rectosphincteric reflex in seven patients who suffered from fecal incontinence. A balloon with a tube attached was inserted into the rectum and inflated at appropriate times to simulate the increase in rectal pressure that occurs when feces are present. A second balloon with a tube attached was positioned at the external sphincter. Its tube went to a device that recorded pressure changes. In normal subjects, slight inflation of the rectal balloon caused contraction of the external sphincter. This response was either very small or completely absent in the seven patients.

Phase 2 was the beginning of biofeedback training to contract the external sphincter as soon as the patient felt the inflation of the rectal balloon. Each session lasted about two hours and included about 50 trials (momentary inflations of the rectal balloon). Biofeedback was provided by permitting the patient to watch the polygraph tracing of the pressure record from the balloon at the external sphincter. He was encouraged to try to contract the sphincter whenever the rectal balloon was inflated and he was praised whenever he produced a normal response. This verbal reinforcement was gradually diminished as normal responses became more frequent. During Phase 3, the final stages of biofeedback training, the patients were trained to make the contractions of the external sphincters more and more similar to normal responses. In addition, during this phase, the patients were weaned from the biofeedback apparatus. That is, during some trials the patients were not permitted to see their tracings on the polygraph.

All of the patients completed their training in four sessions or less. At the time of their report, the investigators had been able to follow up on the status of their patients for periods of six months to five years. Four patients were completely continent. One patient reported rare staining of clothing. Another reported that he is continent at night but sometimes still soils his clothes during the day. The final patient withdrew from the study after the first session.

SECRETION

We now turn to the second of the two physiological processes that take place in the g.i. system—secretion. Two studies have been reported in which normal subjects were taught the use of biofeedback to control their gastric acid secretion.[10] The psychosomatic disorder that immediately comes to mind when we think of stomach acid is ulcers. Might it be possible to alleviate the symptoms of ulcer patients through the use of biofeedback training to reduce their gastric acid secretion?

Welgan[11] conducted two studies with ulcer patients in which he attempted to increase the pH of the stomach. Since pH is a measure of acidity (the lower the value, the greater the acidity), it was logical to try to increase the gastric pH of ulcer patients. In the first experiment ten patients had a pH electrode passed down into their stomach through a nasogastric tube. The electrode was attached to a pH meter which provided visual biofeedback when appropriate. The patients also received auditory feedback in the form of tones which indicated success, that is, that they were increasing their pH. During the course of a session, the patients received an initial 30 minute rest period, followed by three 15 minute biofeedback periods alternated with two additional rest periods. Results indicated that the patients showed a significant increase in gastric pH (the appropriate therapeutic response) from the first 30 minute rest period to the first biofeedback period. However, pH level tended to decline after this during both types of periods.

A second experiment was designed by Welgan to explore further this puzzling finding. Was biofeedback an aid to increasing gastric pH in the first experiment or was there something special about 30 minutes of resting that led to an increase in gastric pH immediately following that time? Two groups of five ulcer patients served in the second experiment. They both had a 30 minute rest period and then Group 1 had 15 minutes additional rest. Group 2, on the other hand, had a 15 minute biofeedback period following their 30 minute rest. Now if biofeedback was an aid to increasing gastric pH, the pH of Group 2 should increase more from minute 31 to 45 than the pH of Group 1. Unfortunately, it did not. Welgan concludes, "This preliminary work suggests that gastric acid secretions may be altered and controlled with the appropriate feedback." We don't feel that such an optimistic view is justified based on Welgan's data, however, we have every reason to believe that, with further technological advances in pH monitoring and feedback, successful applications of biofeedback therapy for ulcer patients will become a reality. As we mentioned above while discussing biofeedback of g.i. motility, the major problem is how to record these relatively slowly changing internal processes.

13

Pain

The first individual began by breaking a 100 watt light bulb, chewing part of it carefully and then swallowing the pieces with a glass of red wine. As if this was not enough, he then pierced his body with three bicycle spokes; one on each side, and the third going through the mouth piercing both the right and left cheek. While this was being performed EEG (electrical activity of the brain recorded from the scalp) and EMG (electrical activity of a muscle recorded from skin surface) recordings were being made. Surprising as it may seem, the spoke going into the right cheek was accompanied by low level muscle activity indicating that this individual was not tense. The EEG record indicated a predominance of alpha wave activity from the back of the head. Even more out of the ordinary was the finding that the puncture wounds healed rapidly with no apparent bleeding or scaring.

There is one aspect of the above report that is missing; this individual reported little or no pain while he was performing these tasks. Why he experienced no pain, and if we too can learn to reduce or modify our own experience of pain, are two of the questions we are going to look at in this chapter.

Scientific research has demonstrated that pain has both a psychological and a physiological component. Given the right conditions, almost any external event can become painful. Not only is it clear that drugs and emotional frame of mind can influence the experience of pain, but research has also shown that just varying the instructions that are given will influence the degree to which one experiences pain. In one such study, telling the subjects to imagine it was a very hot day made it easier to tolerate placing their hands in ice cold water.[1]

One interesting approach to the study of pain was carried out by Ken Pelletier and Eric Peper.[2] These two psychologists studied individuals who were known for their ability to perform an act that we would consider very painful such as sticking a bicycle

spoke through your body, or walking on fire. Hardly the type of exercise any of us would want to go through before breakfast. It was one of their subjects that we described in the first paragraph of this chapter. Of course these individuals are different from the average person who seeks help for pain, but Peper and Pelletier believed that by studying their psychophysiological responses to pain it might be possible to teach others to make similar responses and thus to minimize pain in unavoidable situations.

Since other reports had suggested that yogis may control pain by going into a mental state characterized by alpha waves in their EEG record, Dr. Pelletier decided to test this hypothesis in his work with a second individual known for his ability to control pain. There were two parts to this research. In the first part, the individual was trained to increase alpha and theta waves through the use of biofeedback. In both alpha and theta training this individual did show greater alpha or theta during the biofeedback sessions than he had previously. The second part of the study was designed to determine his physiological reactions to passing a spoke through his arm. He did this three times. Each time before the demonstration, a physician performed a bleeding test in which the standard bleeding time was three minutes. Also the EEG during the bleeding test showed alpha blocking (decrease in alpha) which is characteristic of a normal stress response. However during the puncture demonstrations this individual did not show a decrease in alpha and in fact his alpha appeared to be similar to biofeedback trials in which he did not push the spoke through his arm. Additionally, there was no bleeding apparent at the site of the puncture wound.

These results suggested to Pelletier and Peper that alpha training might be a means for learning pain control. Some initial pilot work was begun in which two individuals were taught to increase alpha through biofeedback techniques. After a period of about seven weeks (30 sessions) these individuals were tested for pain control. Both subjects were instructed to produce alpha while a sewing needle was passed through their hand. The first subject showed no alpha blocking (alpha continued and did not decrease) in the EEG records. Later, this subject reported that there was no pain felt during the session. The other subject did show alpha blocking (and thus could not keep alpha waves predominant) during the session. Interestingly enough, this subject did report pain which suggests that alpha—or the states required to produce alpha—may be involved in the control of pain.

An earlier case report by Linda Gannon and Richard Sternbach had also examined whether alpha training might be useful for controlling pain.[3] This report tells of an individual who in 1964 suffered a head injury. Following this injury, the patient began to have headaches which disappeared within three to four weeks during which time medication had been given. During the next four years, this individual injured his head another four times. Following each injury, headaches came and were relieved through medication except for the last head injury. Two years after this injury, the patient still had headaches, although both neurological and psychiatric examinations had shown no cause. After some months of alpha training (67 sessions) these authors concluded that alpha training itself did *not* alleviate pain. However, in some cases the individual was able to prevent pain by going into an alpha state before his headache began. This is also consistent with the research work with yogis since they were always given painful stimuli after they had begun their meditation.

In one study carried out in India by B. K. Anand, G. S. Chhina and Baldev Singh, two yogis kept their hands in 4° C. water for almost an hour.[4] These yogis claimed to practice a type of meditation called *Raja Yoga* that allowed them to be oblivious to both external and internal environmental stimuli. During the period when the yogis kept their hands in the cold water they reported no discomfort. Psychophysiological measures such as EEG which were taken both before and during the time the yogis had their hands in the water demonstrated a predominance of alpha activity which is consistent with a relaxed rather than a tense state of mind. The general picture from this and the previous studies is that alpha activity may be incompatible with the experience of pain but that going into an alpha state while experiencing pain is not sufficient for reducing the pain.

It was now time to ask if alpha activity is the main ingredient in pain prevention. That is, will just the presence of alpha activity alone be enough to prevent pain or is the alpha activity that is seen in the records a by-product of some other activity which is really the important ingredient in pain reduction? As an illustration, it has been shown that creative scientists often do not have neat and organized offices, but having a messy office will not make one creative. Thus, just the presence of alpha activity in the EEG records of people who can prevent the experience of pain does not mean that it is alpha activity that is responsible for the lack of pain.

Ronald Melzack and Campbell Perry undertook such a study to determine the role of alpha biofeedback training in the treatment of pain.[5] These researchers studied individuals who suffered from chronic pain of pathological origin. Among their subjects were ten who suffered from back pain, four had peripheral nerve injury, three had pain associated with cancer, two had pain associated with arthritis, two had phantom limb pain, two had pain from previous injuries and one had head pain. Before continuing it is important to note that the type of pain dealt with in this study may be different from nonchronic pain such as that experienced while having a tooth filled, putting your hand in cold water as the yogis had done, or even sticking a spoke through your body. What Melzack and Perry did was to divide the patients into three groups. Twelve of the patients received alpha biofeedback training along with hypnotic training instructions. The second group of six received alpha training only and the third group received hypnotic training alone. The hypnotic training began with a set of relaxation instructions which were followed with suggestions to the effect that they were feeling stronger, healthier, having more energy, and that they were emotionally calm and less tense physically and mentally. The alpha training also included a suggestion that the individuals would be able to achieve control over pain.

The results of this study are very interesting. In all three groups, most of the individuals showed an increase in alpha activity which the researchers believed resulted from the training procedure. Even the group that received hypnotic instructions alone showed virtually the same increase in alpha activity over the hypnotic training sessions as the other two groups did over the alpha feedback sessions. However the results related to pain are somewhat surprising. The group that received alpha training plus hypnotic training and the group that received hypnotic training alone both showed a reduction in pain. The group that received alpha training alone showed no such reduction in pain experiences. From this study these researchers concluded that although alpha activity may play a part in pain reduction (the alpha plus hypnosis group showed the greatest pain reduction of all three groups), alpha training alone will not result in a reduction of the pain experience. What will? These researchers suggest that there are four psychological factors that may be important in pain reduction training. First, the individual learns to distract his attention from the painful area. Second, there is a suggestion that the pain will diminish. Third, there is a period of relaxation. And fourth, the individual is brought to believe that he has control over his pain.

At this point we should return to the men with the spokes in their bodies and ask them how they prevent the experience of pain. Again this is from the report by Pelletier and Peper. The first man who chewed light bulbs and stuck spokes through his cheek reported that he has learned to control his fear by dissociating himself from the sensation as he puts the spoke through his skin. He reports that he diverts his awareness of the pain by letting his consciousness drift away and even suggests an exercise to illustrate this. In the exercise, the person imagines a blackboard on which he draws a small square. Within the square, the person then writes 100. Then he or she erases the 100 in his mind and writes 99 within the frame. Then 98 and so forth until the person reaches 0. It is reported that while the counting exercise is going on another person can pinch the person's flesh without pain being experienced. The other subject studied reported a different technique for avoiding pain. He said that since childhood he had learned to ask his body for permission to make a puncture wound. When he feels he has that permission, then he further dissociates himself by viewing the situation as one in which he sticks a needle through *an* arm rather than through *his* arm. Further, both of the individuals studied remarked that pain consists principally of the fear of pain and the attention to the pain and that this can be countered through relaxation and passive attention.

Although the role that biofeedback might play in the reduction of pain is unclear at this time, some pain treatment centers have reported that biofeedback appears useful when combined with other types of treatment.[6] One such facility is the Casa Colina Hospital for Rehabilitative Medicine in Pomona, California. Here the emphasis is on utilizing biofeedback for the treatment of chronic back pain. These clinicians report that even after operations for back pain have been undergone, the person still may be faced with a life of invalidism. In one of their case reports they tell of a woman who five years previously suffered a back injury. When she arrived at the hospital, this woman had gone through five years of pain and three operations for her back problem. She arrived at the hospital in a wheelchair unable to straighten her body. According to the report the first form of treatment was teaching this woman that after a number of years of having others take care of her, she must begin to take care of herself. Thus she was made responsible for keeping track of when to take her medication and getting herself to the dining room. Later, the patient was introduced to biofeedback therapy which she engaged in five times a week for two hours each day. The biofeedback in this case was in relation to EMG activity directed toward teaching the patient to relax. These clinicians report that not only did the original injury bring about tension but also personal problems such as financial difficulties, loss of job, and so forth, which often compound the experience of pain. In the case of the woman reported here, these clinicians reported the remarkable finding that not only was she walking within nine weeks but that she was able to return home and shortly thereafter begin to lead an active life.

Another utilization of biofeedback for the treatment of pain came from the work of Dr. R. H. Gregg and his colleagues. This group was concerned with the pain experienced in childbirth. Expectant mothers were given biofeedback machines which monitored both EMG and GSR (galvanic skin response) activity. During a period of at least four weeks, these mothers were instructed to practice relaxing procedures twice a day with the biofeedback equipment. The mothers who had practiced biofeedback relaxation techniques were then compared with mothers who had not. The results appear promising. The women who received biofeedback training tended to stay in first stage labor a shorter time than those who did not. Also, the need for medication was lower in the biofeedback group.

Presently, it is impossible to evaluate the role of biofeedback alone in pain treatment since few systematic studies have addressed themselves to this area. Those programs that have utilized biofeedback in the treatment of pain such as either treating back pain or pain experienced during childbirth have reported good results. However in both of these cases, the biofeedback training was combined with other factors such as requiring that the patient take responsibility for himself and his or her pain, and instilling a sense of control in the patient. Whether or not biofeedback will prove to be a necessary requirement is still unknown. At this time the real value of biofeedback in terms of pain appears to be that these procedures have allowed medical institutions an avenue for exploring new forms of treatment which leave responsibility and integrity with the patient.

14

Bruxism: Excessive Teeth Grinding

We all grind our teeth together, most of us concentrating this effort three times a day, and many of us clench our teeth a couple of times a day such as while anxiously watching to see if our golf putt will fall into the cup. But some individuals clench or grind their teeth when they are not chewing, swallowing, or playing golf. This excessive, nonfunctional gnashing and grinding of teeth which frequently leads to serious tooth and gum disorders is called bruxism.

Why doesn't the bruxist stop his excessive teeth action since it seems to serve no purpose and is a form of muscular activity over which we do have voluntary control? The bruxist doesn't have this control that most of us possess, just as the overweight overeater can't keep his or her hand out of the refrigerator. A problem which is specific to bruxism is that it commonly occurs at night while the individual is sleeping, often called nocturnal bruxism.

Several years ago it was found that the amount of muscle potential (EMG) recorded from the masseter muscle was highly correlated with the force of biting and chewing. Rugh and Solberg[1] described a portable EMG biofeedback device that was designed to present daytime bruxists with an audible tone when their masseter muscular activity levels exceeded a preset level. Several of the individuals they studied using this instrument reported that they learned to control previously unnoticed oral habits such as excessive clenching and grinding of the teeth. Once again, then, we see how biofeedback helps people to tune into their own bodily responses.

Could such a procedure be used to help the nocturnal bruxist?

Heller and Strong[2] tried using a learning procedure with a nocturnal bruxist. Rather than recording the masseter muscle activity from their subject, they placed a sensitive microphone near his mouth and recorded how many times per minute he ground his teeth. The subject was a 24-year-old graduate student who had suffered from nocturnal bruxism for several years.

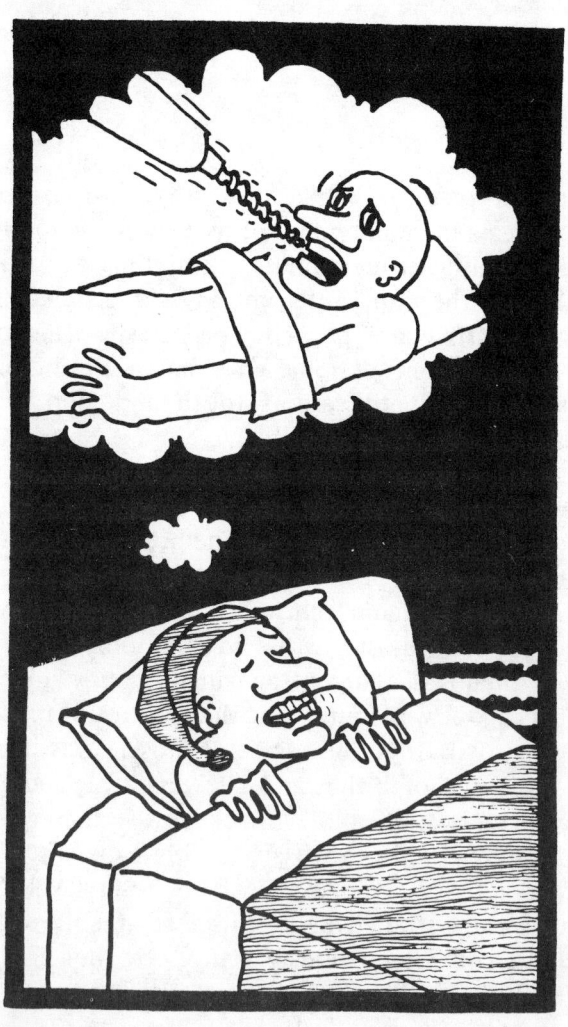

For 18 nights the rate of teeth grinding was recorded and no therapy administered. During this pretreatment phase, the subject ground his teeth an average of 1.75 times per minute. Beginning with the 19th night, every time the subject ground his teeth at the rate of 3 times per five minute interval he was awakened by a noise. During the seven nights of this therapy, he showed on the average 63 percent less grinding than pretreatment. Sounds promising! On the next six nights the subject received no feedback and his grinding increased again. Therapy was started again on the 32nd night and continued until the 52nd night, the conclusion of the study. The average frequency of teeth grinding per minute during this period dropped to 0.4, less than once every two minutes.

In 1975 Rugh and Solberg decided to try using the same EMG biofeedback therapy that had worked for them so well previously for daytime bruxists, with a nocturnal bruxist. They recorded the sleeping masseter activity of a subject before, during, and after biofeedback therapy. The therapy consisted of having a tone alert the sleeping subject whenever muscular activity exceeded a preset level. Before biofeedback treatment the subject made on the average about 30 strong clenchings of the teeth per hour.

Very exciting things happened during biofeedback therapy— those nights during which the subject was hooked up to the alerting system. His masseter activity fell to ten clenches an hour. Unfortunately, when the biofeedback therapy terminated, the average masseter activity went back up to the pretreatment level. We do want to point out here again the importance of following up on any biofeedback treatment to see if the beneficial effects continue after therapy has ended. In the previously described study by Heller and Strong, they also found that on those nights when the subject received no biofeedback, his rate of grinding increased. They, however, went on to give another series of biofeedback treatments and concluded that bruxism could be controlled.

We would have to conclude based on both of these studies that nighttime biofeedback therapy does not work for nocturnal bruxism. On the other hand, we mentioned some research which showed that biofeedback did work for waking bruxism. That is, it enabled the awake bruxist to become aware of chewing and grinding activity to which he was previously unaware and to learn to control these responses in the absence of biofeedback. To us, this is success. Being able to control some behavior only while receiving biofeedback is promising, but it may not be considered therapeutically successful.

Whereas nighttime biofeedback of teeth grinding may not be beneficial to the nocturnal bruxist, other forms of biofeedback may alleviate the condition. It has been found that the degree of bruxism during a particular night is highly correlated with the amount of stress or tension experienced by the individual that day. For example, masseter muscle tension was recorded from a female bruxist for 30 nights. On three of these nights much more clenching and grinding occurred than on the other nights. On the three days preceding these nights she reported the following: job interview, fight with father, quit job. Similar results were obtained from three other nocturnal bruxists studied.

Nonspecific biofeedback to aid in a general reduction of tension has been found to help some bruxists. By nonspecific we mean biofeedback from some location other than the area of the jaw. There have been reports of some nocturnal bruxists being helped through alpha feedback. In these cases, the individuals were given feedback, while awake, to increase the amount of alpha activity in their brain waves. In this way the person learned to lower his or her overall level of tension. At night it was found that these individuals decreased the frequency and severity of their teeth grinding and clenching. Other nocturnal bruxists have been helped in a similar way through the use of daytime biofeedback of muscle tension from the frontalis muscles of the forehead.

One dentist, Dr. Andrew J. Cannistraci,[3] has found that he can cure some nocturnal bruxists with specific muscle potential biofeedback—from the jaw—while they are awake. Perhaps it should not surprise us that previous workers in this area failed to obtain clinically significant relief for nocturnal bruxists through the use of biofeedback from the jaw muscles while the patients were asleep. These patients only received biofeedback when their jaw tension reached some very high level at which point they were awakened. What they missed and what biofeedback should provide for bruxists, is the development of a new awareness and later control of their masseter tension.

Working within this framework, Dr. Cannistraci has been able to help nocturnal bruxists by giving them biofeedback of their jaw muscle tension while they are awake. During the first few sessions, the patient simply learns to recognize varying degrees of tension in his jaw muscle by listening to a tone which varies with his muscle tension. During the second phase of treatment the patient is taught various exercises which enable him to gain control over his jaw tension. That is, he learns to increase and decrease it at will. Once this skill is acquired, he is gradually weaned off the biofeedback so that he will not be dependent on it when he is at home going to sleep in his own bed. Dr. Cannistraci reports that this daytime learning to relax the jaw carries over into the sleeping situation and has provided much relief to several of his nocturnal bruxist patients.

15

Muscle Reeducation

It is erroneous to think of a muscle, such as your bulging bicep, as a single entity all of which contracts or doesn't contract at the same moment in time. The structural unit of a muscle is the muscle fiber, described as a very fine thread, many of which constitute the whole muscle. If we could watch a muscle contract under some kind of magic magnifying glass we would see that rather than all of the fibers contracting together, small groups of them contract at the same moment. And if we were to examine even more closely we would see that all the members of each of these groups of muscle fibers receive their "commands" from a single motor nerve fiber which has come down the spinal cord from the brain. We call the motor nerve fiber and the particular muscle fibers it stimulates a motor unit. The motor unit is, then, the functional entity of muscular activity and not a whole muscle.[1]

Turning now to car accident victims or stroke patients, the reason that they are paralyzed, that their muscles will not work, is that either the appropriate message is not leaving the damaged brain or that the message is being interrupted along the damaged spinal cord. If the damage is repaired quickly, muscular activity is usually regained almost immediately. However, if because of brain or spinal cord injury or disease no messages are sent to a muscle for an extended period of time (several weeks) permanent damage to the muscle may occur.

When we talk about muscle reeducation we are talking about

replacing missing proprioceptive information with biofeedback of the weak but existing electromyographic (EMG) activity from remaining active motor units. Proprioception refers to the information that we normally receive from our muscles concerning where they are and what they are doing.

Marinacci,[2] the first investigator to discuss the use of biofeedback of EMG for muscle reeducation, has reported that sometimes even in cases where it appears that a muscle is totally paralyzed, there remain a few active motor units. There are also sometimes latent motor units which can be reactivated with exercise. With appropriate exercise the latent motor units and the remaining active motor units may increase in strength and control to the point where the muscle becomes useful.

Spinal Cord Injuries

Owen, Toomim, and Taylor,[3] in their informative publication, "Biofeedback of Neuromuscular Re-Education," point out that by using EMG recording they have been able to find active motor units in seemingly paralyzed muscles of more than a dozen individuals with spinal cord injuries. They stress the fact that no matter how severe the damage to the spinal cord, unless it is actually severed, a search should be made with EMG recording for active motor units. Once these active units are found, biofeedback of them serves as a substitute for missing proprioceptive information. Now, with biofeedback and a trained physiotherapist to provide appropriate exercises, the individual can become aware of even slight increases in the activity of the affected muscle. Without biofeedback the patient would probably become discouraged and discontinue the exercises since he would not see or feel any improvement for long periods of time.

Owen et al. describe the progress made by some of the paralyzed patients with spinal cord injury who have been treated at their Biofeedback Research Institute in Los Angeles. Several are working to develop arm extension and hand and finger movement and have shown good progress. Some are working to strengthen trunk muscles. One patient who thought that his spinal cord was completely severed has found a small amount of arm muscle activity and hand movement. A woman who has been slowly regaining muscle function ever since her accident four years ago has found that the use of EMG biofeedback has considerably accelerated her recovery. She now walks a little with no assistance. Owen et al. are quick to caution that muscle reeducation for the spinal cord injured patient is a very slow process requiring probably years of hard work.

Stroke (Cerebral Vascular Accident)

Strokes can result from a blood clot in the brain or a ruptured blood vessel in the brain either of which usually causes complete or partial paralysis on one side of the body. Some stroke patients show no voluntary movement (paralysis) on the involved side but others manifest the opposite problem—too much muscle action on the involved side. Individuals with the latter disorder are called spastic. When a person with normal motor functioning contracts a muscle, another muscle usually relaxes facilitating the movement. However, when the spastic person tries to contract a muscle, the movement is resisted by the inappropriate response of an antagonist muscle.

As with spinal injured persons, biofeedback of EMG can provide stroke patients with substitute information about the contraction of their muscles to replace their lost natural proprioceptive feedback. With the spastic stroke patient it is often necessary to use two EMG units simultaneously since the patient must be trained to increase activity in one muscle and at the same time to decrease activity in another.

John V. Basmajian, Director of the Regional Rehabilitation Research and Training Center in Atlanta, Georgia, and his associates[4] recently published an article summarizing the results of their biofeedback treatment for foot-drop in stroke patients. Foot-drop is a common problem of stroke patients and one which prior to biofeedback often required the patient to wear a short leg brace for correction. You have probably observed a person with foot-drop walking with difficulty dragging the toes on one foot. The paralyzed muscle involved does not permit the ankle to dorsiflex, bend up and back, therefore, the person must walk with the affected foot bent forward.

Twenty stroke victims were used in his investigation. They were treated three times a week for five weeks. During each session the biofeedback group received 20 minutes of therapeutic exercise plus 20 minutes of biofeedback. The control group received 40 minutes of therapeutic exercise. The therapy exercises were the standard rehabilitation procedure. The purpose of the investigation was to see if biofeedback would facilitate recovery from paralytic foot-drop.

Basmajian et al. gave each patient a score based on his or her gait prior to treatment, at the end of training, and at a follow-up examination. The larger the score the more normal the walking. Looking first at Group 1—those patients who received only physical therapy, six out of ten showed some improvement and they still maintained the improvement during the follow-up testing. Note, however, that "3" was the highest score achieved in this group. In the physical therapy plus biofeedback group, Group 2, all subjects showed improvement and maintained it until the follow-up examination. Note that four of the stroke victims in the group improved to the point where their gait was scored "4." And, even more impressive, cases 17 and 19 had worn leg braces prior to training and were able to walk well without them following training. Follow-up testing of these two cases four months and one month after the end of training showed them still to be walking without their braces. Interestingly, case 13 showed even more improvement at his follow-up examination three months after training than he did at the end of training and was able to discard his brace.

Fish, Mayer, and Herman[5] agree that "Biofeedback may be a promising new modality for treatment of neuromuscular disorders," but they challenge Basmajian's basic conclusion based on inadequacies in statistical and research design. Basmajian concluded that for his biofeedback group "the increase in both strength and range of motion was approximately twice as great" as for the group which received only physical therapy. Fish et al. are not questioning the fact that some of Basmajian's patients in his biofeedback group improved to the point where they could throw away their braces. What they are questioning is just what it was in their total treatment which led to their improvement. Only additional work in this field will enable us to determine whether biofeedback per se is the aspect of treatment which makes the difference. This is a very important point and one which could be repeated in almost every chapter of this book.

Richard Herman and his associates[6] at the Moss Rehabilitation Hospital in Philadelphia are also using biofeedback therapy to help stroke victims regain their normal posture and gait. The three biofeedback devices that they are working with are the Limb Load Monitor (LLM), the Step Control Monitor (SCM) and the Knee Position Monitor (KPM).

As you may have noticed, stroke victims who are paralyzed on one side of the body stand in such a way that very little weight is placed on the affected foot. In an effort to correct this imbalance Herman has developed the LLM. This is a pressure sensitive device worn in each shoe. Feedback is in the form of an audible tone which signals to the subject the extent to which he is not bearing his weight equally on both feet. The goals of the project are to improve weight bearing in the affected limb while the patient is standing and, hopefully, walking.[7] Patients worked with a therapist once a week and were required to practice with the LLM at home for at least 30 minutes a day. The first group of patients had severely impaired motor control and none of them showed any improvement in balanced weightbearing. A second group of patients with better initial motor control was more successful in achieving posture control. Four patients with still better motor control not only learned to balance their weight equally on both feet while standing but also improved their walking. The LLM is currently being tested on a large number of paralyzed patients at the Kessler Institute in West Orange, New Jersey.

The SCM and the KPM are in more preliminary stages of development.

Cerebral Palsy

Biofeedback of EMG has been found to be effective in alleviating some of the symptoms of some cerebral palsy patients. For example, Dr. Basmajian and his associates are currently having some success treating foot-drop in cerebral palsy patients.

Finley, Niman, Standley, and Wansley[8] recently reported success using biofeedback of EMG from the forehead in helping four cerebral palsy children. Since cerebral palsy is characterized by spastic movements, too much muscle activity, the investigators rewarded the children for decreasing their forehead EMG. Biofeedback training lasted for six weeks. All four children improved significantly on five oral processing motor skills and three improved their speech significantly. A follow-up examination six weeks after the end of training revealed that all four children had lost their initial gains in speech and motor activity. Six to eight additional EMG biofeedback trials were given and three of the four children quickly showed recovery of their speech and motor function. This is work in progress and it is only a start. If the children can be trained with the EMG biofeedback to the point where they can still maintain their speech and motor behavior without biofeedback a significant contribution will have been made.

Other Neuromuscular Disorders

The use of EMG biofeedback with children who were poliomyelitis patients was briefly referred to in Chapter 4. This work was done in the 1950s before the term "biofeedback" was coined and before much was known about training individual motor units. But limited success was achieved with some of the children because of the rewarding aspects of the particular display which was used, a clown's face. More recently Marinacci has reported partial success with 20 polio patients. He points out again, and we think that this is worth repeating, that even in extremely paralyzed muscles there may still exist a few active motor units. And proper exercise, guided by EMG recording may increase the frequency and strength of these motor units to the point where the muscle becomes functional again.

Torticollis, also known as wryneck, is a neuromuscular disorder in which the head turns to one side. Some investigators are trying simultaneous EMG biofeedback from both sides of the neck. In this way the patient learns to decrease muscle activity on the overactive side and increase activity on the other side. A physical therapist working with torticollis patients commented that it sometimes appears that the patient has an emotional need to allow the condition to continue. This can be true of any apparently physical disorder and this is why psychological counseling is often just as important as the physical therapy.

Summary

We trust that mention of the preliminary work in this chapter will not raise false hopes in individuals afflicted with these diseases and their families. We only want you to be aware that a small group of psychologists, engineers, physical therapists, and medical doctors are starting to investigate the uses of EMG biofeedback in the treatment of neuromuscular disorders.

At this time, most people are unaware of the success that a few have achieved with biofeedback. A 38-year-old male stroke victim was told at a rehabilitation center that he would never show much improvement; that is, he would always have a spastic arm and shoulder and would not regain voluntary control. The goal of this man as expressed to a psychologist at a biofeedback clinic is to approach the individual who examined him at the rehabilitation center, bring thumb to nose, and wiggle fingers in a widely known gesture!

16

Control of Paralyzed or Artificial Limbs

In the previous chapter on muscle reeducation we mentioned the work of Basmajian who has been using biofeedback to aid partially paralyzed patients, usually stroke victims, who were suffering from foot-drop. He used biofeedback to "reeducate" the neuromuscular system involved to the point where the individual can, once again, produce dorsal flexion of the affected foot.

Another approach to aiding individuals with paralyzed limbs is to apply an external electric shock to the muscle or the nerve leading to the muscle. Here the external stimulation replaces the missing internal stimulation to the muscle that normally occurs in nonparalyzed people. This general procedure is called functional electrical stimulation (FES). Dr. James Reswick and his associates at the Rancho Los Amigos Hospital in Downey, California are using this approach to treat patients with motor neuron diseases. Their goal is to reutilize diseased or damaged muscles and nerves through the use of FES. In some cases it has been found that after repeated external stimulation, the individual begins to regain the use of the muscle and is able to once again use it without braces and without further FES.

Let us describe for you the use of FES with foot-drop patients and then we will see where and how biofeedback fits into this approach.

The use of FES in the rehabilitation of patients with paralyzed limbs was first introduced by Liberson, Holmquest, Scott and Dow in 1961.[1] Figure 3 depicts the basic setup used with foot-drop patients. An electric stimulator was located in the patient's pocket. Two wires coming from it led to electrodes which were attached

FIGURE 3

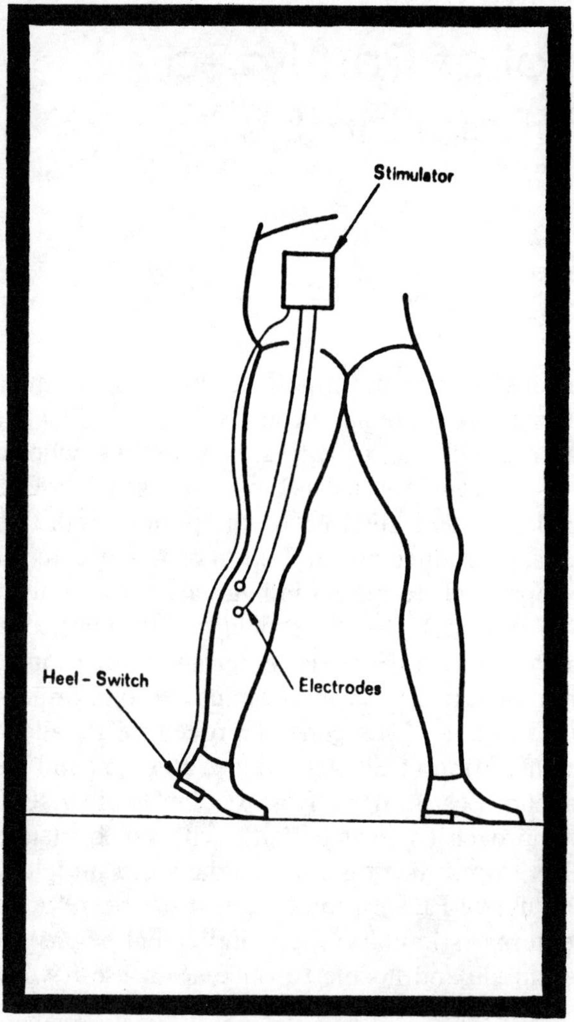

Source: L. Vodovnik. "Information Processing in the Central Nervous System during Functional Electrical Stimulation." In C. W. Caldwell (Ed.), *Development of Orthotic Systems Using Functional Electrical Stimulation and Myoelectric Control.* Ljubljana, Yugoslavia: University of Ljublijana, Laboratory for Medical Electronics and Biocybernetics, 1971.

to the skin over the common peroneal nerve behind the knee. This is the nerve that normally carries the internal signal which brings about dorsal flexion of the foot. The crucial problem was what to use as a switch so that the stimulation would get to the peroneal nerve just at the right time—when the individual started to take a step. The clever solution, as you can see in the figure, was to place the switch in the heel of the patient's shoe. Whenever the patient lifted his foot, the switch in his heel activated the electrical stimulator which sent a signal to the electrodes over the peroneal nerve resulting in dorsal flexion and the desired lifting of the foot.

One difficulty with the above system is that a wire is visible extending from the heel switch up to the electrical stimulator. This may not seem important to a nonparalyzed person, but to a paralyzed patient the appearance of any assistive device is very important. One approach to overcome this has been to develop wireless broadcasting of the triggering signal from the heel to the stimulator.

A second method of dealing with the problem brings us to an application of biofeedback that didn't work. This procedure involved picking up EMG signals from the patient's back and using them to trigger the stimulator. The EMG wires would be covered by clothing and, therefore, acceptable to most patients. Sounds good so far! Very early in the development of this system it was determined that if you use biofeedback training to teach an individual with foot-drop to contract a certain muscle in his back he can do it. But, if he tries to do it just as he starts each and every step, which is what is necessary, the psychological problem becomes worse than the paralysis. Therefore, it was concluded that an automatically triggering EMG system was necessary. To accomplish this, the investigators had to locate a muscle in the back which naturally contracted at the point in time when dorsal flexion of the foot was desired. This they did with some time and effort. At this point the complete device was constructed including the elaborate electronic circuit necessary to filter and process the EMG signal and delay it until just the right moment. When it was tried on the first patient it didn't work reliably. Another patient with foot-drop was brought in and the device tried on him. Again, it didn't work reliably enough to be useful. Why not? What went wrong between the research laboratory and the clinical application? It turns out that the EMG signals recorded from the muscles in the back of a partially paralyzed patient with foot-drop are very different than those recorded from nonparalyzed individuals and the latter were used in the development of the device. The foot-drop patients lack the synchrony between the activity of the muscles of the back and walking which is found in other people.

An entirely different method of helping individuals to move paralyzed limbs is to provide a motorized brace, or orthotic, which when attached to the limb and activated, moves it.

Moe and Schwartz[2] working with an electric arm aid have come up with a clever control system. They use the patient's eye movements to signal the electric arm aid in which direction it should move the patient's paralyzed arm. And the rate of movement of the eyes is used to control the rate of movement of the hand. If the patient wants to just look around, he simply gives two rapid blinks which turns off his arm aid. Two more blinks turn it back on. The complete system makes use of a small computer and is, obviously, quite complicated and expensive but it does show promise for helping those patients who are almost completely paralyzed and, therefore, without other effective muscular control sites.

Biofeedback of eye movements must be used with patients who are going to use the arm aid system so that they can learn to achieve precise control over the position of their eyes. In Figure 4 we have reproduced an example of eye "writing" to demonstrate the degree of control that is possible with practice.

The first EMG controlled prosthesis, or artificial limb, was produced in 1948, however, several years passed before the device was ready for clinical application. When we talk about "EMG controlled" artificial limbs we do not mean that an existing healthy muscle is used by itself to move a prosthetic device. Rather, as in the FES systems discussed above, the electrical signal given off by the contraction of an existing muscle is used to *trigger* the movement of an artificial limb. The movement is actually brought about through the use of small electric motors concealed in the prosthetic. The recent technological advances that have been made in miniaturization of the necessary mechanical and electrical components have made possible the development of self-contained, cosmetically acceptable artificial limbs.

FIGURE 4

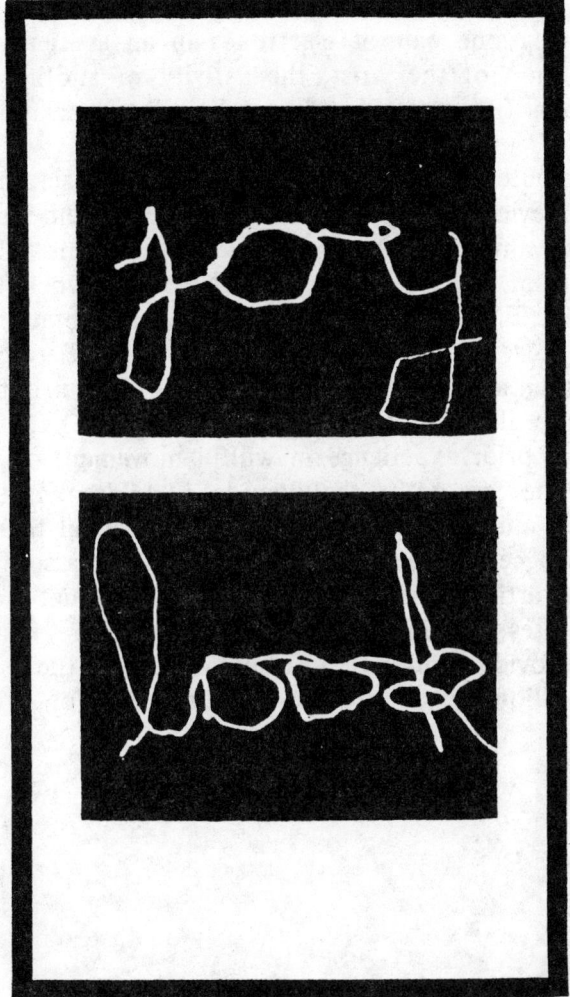

Source: M. L. Moe and J. T. Schwartz. "Ocular Control of the Rancho Electric Arm." In M. M. Gavrilovic and A. B. Wilson, Jr. (Eds.), *Advances in External Control of Human Extremities.* Belgrade: Yugoslav Committee for Electronics and Automation, 1973.

In many cases the EMG electrodes are built right into the socket of the artificial limb. Muscle potential from the stump which is picked up by one pair of electrodes in an artificial arm may trigger rotation of the wrist, the activity of another pair may control elbow flexion while still a third pair triggers movement of the fingers.

Many amputees require little training, biofeedback or other, to use such a device. Since their central nervous system is still intact, when they want to, for example, rotate their wrist, the correct signals go from their brain down to their stump where they interface with the EMG electrodes which trigger the rotation. In some amputees, however, the signals reaching the EMG electrodes in the socket of their artificial limb are not so clear. This may be because of the nature of the surgery used in removing the limb or because of a lack of prior experience in willful movement of the limbs, such as is the case with "thalidomide"[3] children. In such cases biofeedback must be used to teach the individual that the contraction of a certain remaining muscle results in a specific movement of the artificial limb. It should be realized that the amputee not only loses certain muscles but also sensory systems that normally provide him with information about the position of his limbs. Biofeedback provides a substitute for this missing information.

17

Teaching Deaf Children to Speak

Before we begin our discussion of how biofeedback has been used to help children who were born deaf learn to speak, we want to mention briefly why we chose this topic rather than deafness later in life, or blindness or some other sensory impairment to discuss in detail.

Many devices have been designed in recent years to help blind people or almost blind people receive information about the visual world. The simplest example would be thick eye glasses or contact lenses which help by altering the incoming visual stimulus, that is, they aid someone with very poor vision by helping to focus incoming light on the appropriate part of the eye. If someone is totally blind then the incoming visual signals must be converted to some other sensory modality such as hearing. This can be done in a variety of ways, for example, the tapping of a cane can be used by a blind person to avoid obstacles in his path. But what if the blind individual needs more information than simply whether or not he is approaching an obstacle?

One device that is currently being developed makes use of two tiny television cameras mounted on the blind person's head much like eye glasses.[1] The picture that is received, that is, whatever is in front of the person, is electronically converted into a tactile image that he feels on the skin of his stomach. For example, this device could conceivably be used by a blind person working on an assembly line where he had to attach one of three possible wheels depending upon which one of three possible parts went by. On the skin of his stomach he would feel an outline in the shape of the part going by and thereby make the correct decision. This visual aid could be used just as effectively by people who are both blind and deaf.

Haig Kafafian has been working on a system to help such individuals, blind and deaf, to communicate.[2] His system makes use, again, of the sense of touch. The blind-deaf person wears a special harness against the skin of his abdomen to which are attached eight small vibrators on the left side and eight on the right. With this system you can communicate with a person by depressing the appropriate keys based on a special code, on a 16-key keyboard which then causes the appropriate vibrators to move. As long as both individuals have been properly trained and know the code, it doesn't matter if one or even both have lost their sight and/or hearing.

We consider the devices described above and others that you have probably thought of, such as hearing aids, to be examples of feedback but not necessarily biofeedback. We think that you will agree, however, that the system we are about to describe for teaching deaf children to speak is an example of biofeedback.

Why is it so difficult for children who are born deaf to learn to speak normally? There are two related reasons. They don't hear (receive auditory feedback) other speakers and they don't receive auditory feedback of their own attempts to speak.

How successful are current procedures for teaching deaf children to speak? Various workers in this field give differing views ranging from extremely positive to quite negative. In a talk to a UNESCO seminar on special education for handicapped children in 1968, Hansen pointed out that while few deaf children learn to talk well enough to be understood by everyone, and many acquire almost no speech at all, most fall somewhere between these extremes: they acquire enough speech to be understood with difficulty, at least by close acquaintances.

There is a great deal of evidence that the experience of hearing speech plays a key role in the development of one's ability to produce speech. Therefore, whenever possible corrective action such as surgery, fitting with a hearing aid and so on should be taken to provide the child with maximal auditory feedback.

In some cases where a child has slight hearing, visual aids can be used to supplement his available feedback. In one experiment reported by Boothroyd[3] two groups of subjects—one group more deaf than the other—were given visual help in producing speech of a certain pitch. That is, the subjects' speech was recorded, processed by a computer and then fed back to them via a visual display so that they could see rather than hear how close they were coming to producing the desired speech. Both groups improved during practice with the visual display. Perhaps, the more interesting finding was that the group of subjects with partial hearing continued to show improvement in the pitch control of their speech after the visual training ended. The author stated: "It was almost as though in the case of the less deaf, visual training had attuned them to auditory-feedback cues which had taken over the role of controlling pitch." We think that this might be analogous to what happens in other forms of biofeedback training discussed earlier in this book such as therapy for blood pressure control. While the individual is receiving biofeedback he becomes aware of or sensitive to internal bodily cues to which he previously did not attend. This is the essence of how biofeedback helps someone once they are unhooked from the biofeedback equipment.

What about the child who is totally deaf; what forms of biofeedback might be used to help him learn to speak? As was mentioned above, displays, usually visual, have been used. These may be thought of as patterns on a TV screen. Such displays have two functions. The first is to give a child a pattern, which represents some feature such as pitch or loudness of an utterance, which he is to attempt to match. Usually the teacher will produce the pattern by making the desired utterance. Ideally, the training display should continue to show a visual representation of the teacher's utterance while the student attempts to produce a matching pattern. The second function of the display is, of course, to provide objective feedback to the deaf student and the teacher.

The next question is what generates or controls the visual displays? That is, what is recorded from the child? It is speech, you answer, and it is recorded with a microphone. That is one possibility, but there are other measures related to speech that have been used for picking up specific aspects of the speech signal.

To obtain a measure of pitch or nasalization, a tiny accelerometer taped to the throat or nose has been used. Other methods of recording nasalization have included measurement of air flow through the nose and the acoustic energy radiated from the nostrils. The degree of nasalization is a common problem in the speech of deaf people since it depends upon the control of the soft palate which functions as a gate between the oral and nasal cavities. Some sounds are more nasal than others, examples of nasal consonants are "M" and "N." It is very difficult for a deaf child to learn to control the opening and closing of his soft palate since he can't see it in other speakers and because he receives very little direct feedback from it.

Additional measures of parts of the speech apparatus have included recording the activity of the vocal folds in the throat and recording the electromyographic activity of the tongue and lips. The major difficulty with both of these procedures is that they interfere with the speech process.

We will now describe a computer-based system of speech training for deaf children developed by R. S. Nickerson, K. N. Stevens and their associates at Bolt Beranek and Newman, Inc. Speech information from a microphone and an accelerometer is fed to a computer and stored in its memory. The content is continually updated with the most recent two seconds of speech always in storage. It is this information that is used to generate various visual displays.

Figure 5 on the left-hand side shows a trial in which a child was successful in producing speech of the desired pitch or frequency (note the smile in the upper right hand corner of Frame d). Since this work is being done with children, an effort was made to develop a gamelike situation that they would find interesting. The object of the game is for the child to get all of the balls, which can be seen in the lower left corner of the display, into the basket. As the child speaks, the ball begins to move towards the basket, its height being a function of the pitch of the child's voice.

The instructor can train the child to raise or lower his pitch by raising or lowering the opening in the wall through which the ball must pass just prior to falling in the basket. The teacher can also become more demanding, that is, require more exact pitch, by making the opening in the wall smaller. In the right-hand side of the same figure the child's pitch was too high as depicted by the ball hitting above the opening in the wall.

FIGURE 5

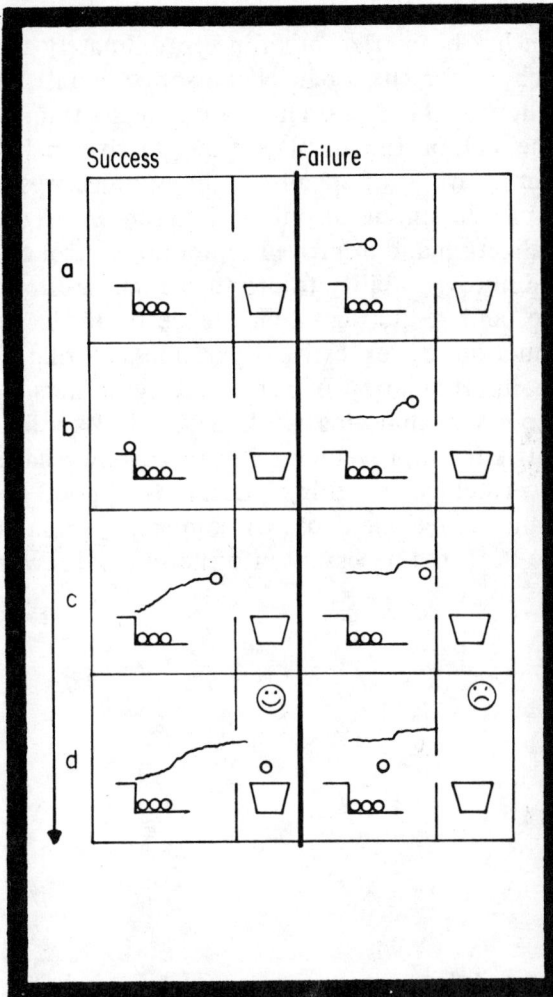

Source: Adapted from R. S. Nickerson and K. N. Stevens, "Teaching Speech to the Deaf: Can a Computer Help?" *IEEE Transactions on Audio and Electroacoustics,* 1973, AU-21, 445-55.

This same display can be used to teach appropriate loudness to a deaf child. In this case the size of the ball is determined by the loudness of the child's speech. If he speaks too loudly the ball will get too large to fit through the opening in the wall. The display could be used for other measures of speech activity such as nasality or tongue position.

This system has been tried out for approximately two years at the Clarke School for the Deaf. Nickerson summarized its effectiveness as follows: "These data indicate that the training that was done with the aid of the display was effective in helping deaf students attain a variety of specific training objectives such as the following: improved timing of phrases and sentences; reduction of excessive nasalization and improved temporal control of the velum (soft palate); improved ability to produce a fall in pitch at the end of a sentence, and reduction of incidence of inadvertent jumps in pitch; reduction of excessive breathiness during phonation; improvements in articulation of some specific sounds." Nickerson points out, however, that this work is still in its infancy and to date (1976) striking improvements in intelligibility have not been obtained. Nevertheless, we think that it is a good example of biofeedback and an excellent use of computer-generated displays which provide both the necessary information and rewards for the user.

18

Stuttering

With a carefully customized biofeedback training program, we believe that higher success rates can be achieved with stutterers than those usually obtained with more conventional therapy in which a third are cured, a third improve and a third remain unchanged.

The features of stuttering are involuntary, audible or silent repetition or prolongation of sounds, syllables, and brief words. Stuttering usually begins in childhood between 18 months and nine years of age. It comes on gradually, not suddenly and is a problem for approximately one percent of the school-age population. The incidence of speech disfluency or stuttering has been estimated to be from two to five times more common in males than in females.

In a sense all of us stuttered at one time, but most of us showed less and less disfluency as our language abilities developed. As a baby you probably pleased your proud parents on many occasions by saying da-da-da-da-da or some such repetition of sound. Wyatt[1] points out that children tend to repeat the unit of speech that is characteristic of their particular level of language development. The very young babbling baby repeats sounds, later he will repeat simple words and eventually short phrases. One study revealed that the peak of disfluency usually occurs during the third year. After that, in general, as a child grows older, there is a decrease in repetitions.

Why is it that some people never outgrow this repetition of sounds when they talk? And why did other stutterers speak with normal fluency for several years and only start stuttering at, for example age eight? And why do some stutterers speak with normal fluency sometimes but not at other times? Unfortunately, the same answer must be given to all of these questions: we don't know.

One common characteristic of many stutterers is that they were late to speak. An interesting observation, however, by Johnson et al.[2] was that the mothers of stutterers tended to indicate that their children were "much slower than average" in acquiring speech but in actuality the average age at which they started to talk was not different than the age at which his control group, a group of nonstutterers, began to talk. This tells us something about one of the very important factors in the development of stuttering—the reactions of parents to the speech of their children.

An examination of data from different cultures reveals some interesting information about the role of stress in stuttering. According to Gregory[3] there is more stuttering in competitive, status-conscious societies. For example, there is very little stuttering in Polynesian societies but a high incidence in Japan.

You might have noticed the effect of stress or anxiety on a friend who stutters. In a relaxed atmosphere where just the two of you are talking, your friend might not stutter. But when your friend finds himself in a tense situation, he may stutter a great deal.

If you have observed a friend or someone else while they are stuttering, you may have noticed that the disfluency is often accompanied by grimaces, tics, and other signs of heightened muscle tension in the face and/or neck. Before proceeding to describe the use of biofeedback to aid stutterers, permit us to describe for you the use of biofeedback to help an individual who suffered from, among other things, high levels of tension in his throat and facial muscles.

The following case was described in a recent article by LeVee, Cohen and Rickles.[4] The patient was hospitalized suffering from alcoholism, drug addiction and, the symptoms that are relevant to our current discussion, tightness of his jaw and a constriction of his throat. These latter symptoms interfered with his career as a successful musician, and led to financial difficulties and marital problems. He first noticed that he was having an abnormal tightening of his jaw, throat, and face muscles in 1955. His speech became less fluent and his performance as a musician degenerated so that he had to play second chair parts, and only on occasional calls. During this period he started drinking heavily, taking Dexamyl tablets, and trying different types of psychotherapy. He tried Freudian-type therapy, hypnotherapy, mood elevating drugs and behavioral psychotherapy. Nothing seemed to help his muscle tension problem and just prior to being hospitalized, he was drinking a pint to a quart of vodka an evening and taking 10-15 Dexamyl tablets a day.

Following an extensive examination in the V.A. hospital it was decided that the cause of the unusually high muscle tension was some underlying emotional disturbance. The treatment decided upon was a combination of psychotherapy aimed at helping the patient deal with his anxiety-producing conflicts and biofeedback aimed at reducing tension in the muscles of the face and throat. At this point we would like to point out that in strict Freudian-type therapy only underlying causes of the tension would have been dealt with and in strict behaviorally oriented therapy only the excessive muscle tension would have been dealt with. Remember, both of these therapies had been tried previously on the patient and had failed when presented separately. The new psychotherapy sessions were directed at helping the patient recognize and discuss his underlying feelings of inadequacy and hostility towards his wife, brothers, and father, all of whom were good musicians. The psychotherapy was started first and the patient made such good progress that he was released from the hospital. He started experiencing increasing constriction in his mouth and throat muscles. Biofeedback training was now initiated.

For the first three biofeedback sessions the patient was taught to reduce the muscle tension in his frontalis muscle. The feedback display used consisted of a column of seven lights, each representing an equal number of microvolts of muscle tension. If, for example, at the beginning of a session the tension from the patient's forehead was 70 microvolts, then each light would represent 10 microvolts and the patient's task would be to put out as many lights as possible by lowering his muscle potential. As we have mentioned previously when discussing symptoms such as tension headaches, reduction of tension in the frontalis muscle usually brings about a general feeling of relaxation. For the next three sessions electrodes were placed on the skin over the throat (larynx) and biofeedback again used to teach muscle relaxation.

Fourteen additional sessions were conducted during which the patient while still receiving biofeedback from his throat muscles was instructed alternately to play his flute and then relax his throat muscles as much as possible. He very quickly learned to maintain a normal muscle potential level both prior to playing and immediately after playing. Follow-up studies of the patient for six months have indicated that he is still free of his muscle tension problem nor has there been any shift of tension to another area. Following the biofeedback therapy, the patient advanced from third to first-chair positions on three instruments and has been performing solo parts with no discomfort.

Levee, Cohen and Rickles, the authors of the article describing this case, stress, and we would agree, that biofeedback was successful in this instance when used as an *adjunct* to psychotherapy. This means that biofeedback if used alone or at an early stage in the history of the disorder might not have helped. But biofeedback when used together with more conventional psychotherapy did bring about the desired results.

Returning now to the treatment of stuttering with biofeedback of muscle potentials, two relevant articles have recently appeared. In the first, Hanna, Wilfling and McNeill[5] describe their work with a 19-year-old student who had been a severe stutterer for ten years. In their rationale for using EMG (electromyogram) biofeedback, the authors mention that many researchers believe that stuttering is accompanied by a spasm of the laryngeal muscles. They felt that if biofeedback will help a stutterer to reduce his laryngeal muscle tension, perhaps it will reduce his stuttering. Well, did it?

First, let's note the procedure used to provide biofeedback. Muscle potential electrodes were attached to the skin of the patient's neck over the larynx. Feedback of muscle tension was provided in the form of a tone that increased in frequency in proportion to the amount of EMG activity. The patient was told that the greater the tension in his speech muscles, the higher the pitch of the tone. He was instructed to produce a low-frequency tone as often as possible.

The patient became familiar with the EMG biofeedback equipment by practicing tensing and relaxing his throat, swallowing, and so forth. According to the authors of the article, he very quickly got so good at the task that he was able to play the tone like a musical instrument. Next he was asked to describe some pictures that the therapist showed to him. He was told that the biofeedback equipment would be turned on and off while he spoke. The session was divided into four talking periods, each nine minutes, and biofeedback was presented during the first and third periods.

The patient's baseline percent syllables stuttered, the amount of stuttering he did prior to biofeedback training, was approximately 18. While the patient was receiving biofeedback there was a clear decrease in the amount of stuttering. When the feedback was turned off, the average amount of stuttering increased. Once again there was a decrease in stuttering while the patient was receiving biofeedback and finally another increase in stuttering when biofeedback was removed. The results for muscle potential activity were quite similar. That is, EMG from the throat decreased during biofeedback, increased when the biofeedback was turned off, decreased again when it was turned on and, finally, increased when it was turned off again. The authors of the article point out that these data provide evidence that stuttering and laryngeal tension are intimately related and that by reducing the latter the former may be reduced.

This is all well and good for a laboratory worker to say—EMG biofeedback from the throat reduced stuttering. But, as we have pointed out before, for any type of therapy to be clinically significant its effects must endure long after the biofeedback device is turned off. This certainly wasn't the case here. In defense of the investigators who carried out this work, they point out that perhaps with an extensive treatment program stressing transfer and maintenance of fluency, stutterers could learn to attend to subtle internal cues of laryngeal tension in the absence of biofeedback equipment and thereby learn to control their disfluency.

Florence Myers[6] in a dissertation study conducted in our laboratory at Penn State, examined the assumption that EMG activity from the throat is the best physiological measure to use when providing biofeedback to stutterers. How might you determine the most appropriate measure? Dr. Myers looked at respiration, skin conductance, vasomotor activity, heart rate, and EMG from the throat of 20 stutterers at the point in time immediately before they spoke. What she was looking for, more precisely, was a change in any of the physiological measures that occurred for a particular subject immediately prior to stuttering but not prior to a fluent utterance. This, then, would be the logical response to use in biofeedback training sessions with that particular stutterer. She began the study asking why should we assume that EMG from the throat is the most appropriate response and why should we assume that the best response to work with for one stutterer will necessarily be the best response to use with another stutterer. In general, her results supported her expectation. When the data from all 20 subjects were combined, EMG from the throat did not show the greatest change immediately prior to stuttering, and there was a great deal of individual difference in just which physiological response did show the largest change prior to stuttering.

Guitar,[7] in the first part of a two-part study, decided to investigate the effect of biofeedback training to reduce tension in other muscles in addition to the throat on stuttering. His three subjects had pairs of EMG electrodes placed over their lips, under the chin, over the frontalis muscle and on the throat. A tone which changed in frequency with muscle tension was used to provide biofeedback. The stutterers were trained to lower their muscle tension separately for each of the four muscles involved prior to speaking. The investigator then compared separately for each stutterer and each of the four muscles the decrease in muscle tension and the decrease in stuttering.

The first stutterer could reduce his lip EMG the most (75 percent) and, correspondingly, he showed the greatest decrease in stuttering while receiving lip EMG biofeedback (88 percent). The second stutterer was most successful in reducing the EMG from his larynx (55 percent) and, again, correspondingly, it was during this training that he showed his biggest decrease in stuttering (24 percent). The third stutterer showed the greatest reduction in EMG from both his lip and chin muscles (86 and 75 percent). His biggest reduction in stuttering occurred during biofeedback training from his lip and larynx (57 and 56 percent).

Guitar concluded from his results that preutterance muscular activity is associated with stuttering. The particular muscle which seems to be most highly related varies, however, from stutterer to stutterer. This is similar to Myers' finding that each stutterer seems to show a characteristic anticipatory physiological change immediately prior to stuttering.

What do these results say to the speech therapist or psychologist who is thinking about using biofeedback training to help a patient who stutters? We think that these results should be encouraging but the lesson to be learned is that the biofeedback training must be customized for each stutterer. First, the therapist must determine which physiological response shows the greatest change for the patient immediately prior to stuttering. Then, using feedback of that response, meaningful biofeedback training sessions can proceed.

19

Alertness

When Ben Franklin felt himself getting drowsy but wanted to remain alert, such as when reading late at night, he held a bottle of expensive whiskey over the hard floor. Fear of dropping the bottle and wasting the good whiskey kept him ever vigilant.[1]

Vigilance or alertness refers to our ability to respond to incoming signals. By signals we mean all those things that we see, hear, feel, smell, and taste which require us to respond in some way. For example, did you notice, and respond appropriately to that quick frown when one of your poker-playing friends looked at his last card?

It has been known for many years that a drowsy or fatigued person performs poorly on any type of alertness or vigilance task. When we speak of vigilance tasks, we are not just talking about laboratory experiments. We are talking about common problems such as driving on a highway when you have been on the road for many hours, or a pilot who has been flying from Rome to New York and has been in the air for nine hours. We are talking about the ship's captain, the railroad engineer, or the long-haul truck driver all of whom must remain alert for very long periods of time. We are concerned about anybody in a situation who must be alert to incoming stimuli in the face of drowsiness, fatigue and boredom. Other workers for whom alertness is a problem would include assembly-line workers in a factory, surgeons who have been operating for many hours without a break, air traffic controllers, and even diplomats about to make important decisions concerning our life and death under less than optimal conditions of alertness.

What can biofeedback contribute to the problem of alertness? Let us redescribe this problem as it was first discussed by the German physiologist Kornmuller.[2] During the closing phases of World War II, German scientists were busily working on an automatic device for alerting personnel such as pilots when they were in a dangerous condition with regard to drowsiness or fatigue. Kornmuller developed what was an ingenious biofeedback system. At that time, of course, we didn't have the concept of "biofeedback," but we think you will agree that this was a very clever biofeedback device.

He used brain wave recordings as a physiological indicator of the alertness of the subject. We can tell from the frequency and amplitude of a person's brain waves when he or she is becoming sleepy. Figure 6 shows typical patterns of brain waves for alert, drowsy, and sleeping subjects. Kornmuller's device caused an alarm to ring whenever the German pilot's brain waves indicated that he was entering into a drowsy state. And as soon as the pilot regained his alert state, the alarm terminated. The report of this work in Germany caused the U.S. government to support research dealing with the feasibility of this device. The work to be described next was carried out at Tufts University in the late 1940s and early 1950s under the supervision of John L. Kennedy.

Kennedy[3] referred to the device he worked on as an alertness indicator. In the first phase of the project he tried to use a brain wave apparatus in the laboratory. He gave his subjects a monotonous vigilance task and recorded their EEG (electroencephalogram) from four locations on the head simultaneously. Two facts emerged from these initial observations. The first was that the range of individual differences in patterns of EEG that seemed to relate to drowsiness was tremendous. That is, where one subject's EEG was of a certain frequency and amplitude when he became drowsy, a second subject showed quite a different pattern when he became drowsy and so on. The second problem observed was that many different things in addition to how drowsy you are affect your EEG; for example, having a relaxing thought versus

FIGURE 6

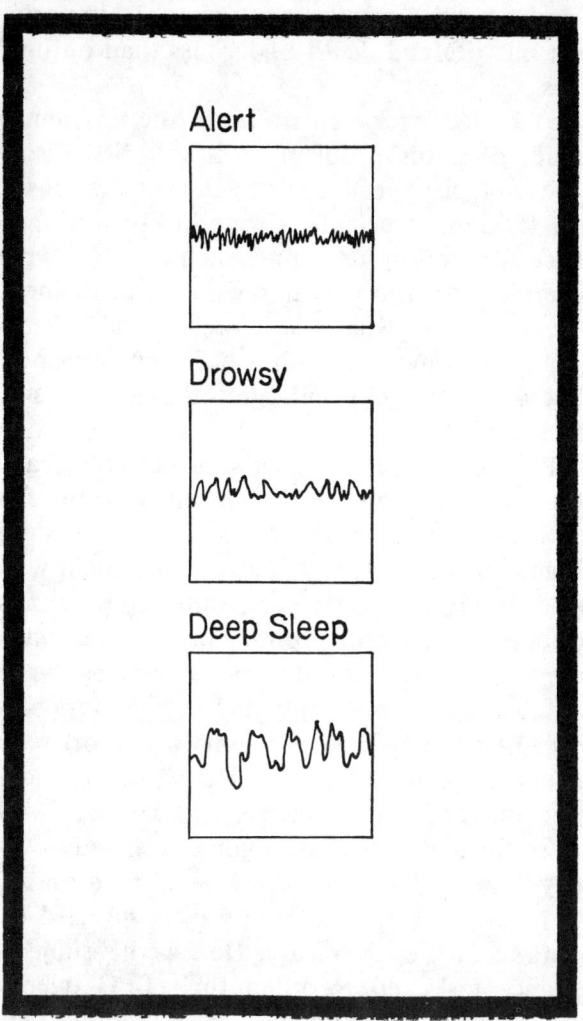

worrying about performing well on the task at hand will yield very different EEGs.

These problems caused Kennedy to abandon the EEG for a different physiological indicator of alertness. He selected the electromyograph, or muscle potentials as they are sometimes called, as his alternative indicator of alertness. In his first EMG

experiment he tried using electrodes on two parts of the arm: biceps and triceps. Unfortunately, these locations did not yield muscle potentials that varied systematically with alertness. He concluded that these large muscles of the body were more or less "silent" unless they were involved in much more physical action than was required for most vigilance tasks.

Next Kennedy tried placing muscle potential electrodes on the pinna, the outer part of the ear. His results were much more promising. From this new location he obtained muscle potentials which varied with readiness to respond to a signal. That is, subjects took much longer to respond to a signal that was presented when they were producing low muscle potentials from their pinnas.

In the next series of experiments, Kennedy tried using EMG electrodes on the forehead. An alarm was hooked up to the apparatus so that it would sound if the subject's forehead muscle potential fell below a preset level. It stayed on until the muscle potential increased.

Kennedy's alertness indicator was never actually put to use primarily because of practical considerations. At the time that this work was done, early 1950s, the available amplifiers and recording devices were very bulky and heavy. Therefore, the equipment necessary to awaken a drowsy pilot, or truck driver, or railroad engineer was really too burdensome. Now equipment which would do the same job could be built into a very small package weighing only a few ounces.

Recently, investigators working with more sophisticated equipment have returned to the problem of relating a specific pattern of physiological activity to alertness. James O'Hanlon[4] of Human Factors Research, Inc., found that the amount of theta activity— brain waves with a frequency between 4-7 Hz.—recorded from the occipital area (the back of the head) was the best indicator of vigilance behavior. The more theta activity, the poorer a subject's performance.

Building on this finding, Beatty, Greenberg, Deibler and O'Hanlon[5] decided to see (1) if they could use biofeedback to manipulate the amount of theta produced and (2) if suppression of theta would result in more efficient performance, and augmentation of theta worse than normal performance. Each subject was trained in two separate one-hour EEG biofeedback sessions. Half the subjects were trained to suppress theta and half to augment theta. If you were in the suppress group, a tone would signal to you that you were doing the right thing if you showed less theta from one second to the next. If you were in the augmentation group, the same tone would signal to you that you were doing the right thing if you increased theta from one second to the next. Through the use of biofeedback, both groups were successful in manipulating the amount of theta produced. Now, to turn to the second question: What did this do to the vigilance performance of the two groups?

The exciting finding was that those subjects who had been taught to suppress theta showed almost no performance decrement during a two-hour monotonous vigilance task. On the other hand, the performance of those subjects who augmented their theta production deteriorated rapidly. To the best of our knowledge at this time nobody has followed up on this research.

Two questions that we asked ourselves after becoming familiar with this work are (1) Could you train individuals who must perform vigilance type tasks under fatiguing conditions, for example, pilots, to suppress theta and have the beneficial effect on their performance be long-lasting or must you give them biofeedback of theta while they are performing their vigilance task? The latter was done in the above laboratory experiment. (2) If theta activity is such an accurate indicator of vigilance performance and individuals must be given biofeedback of theta suppression to prevent deterioration of their vigilance performance, then why not design a new alertness indicator, a device which will ring an alarm whenever the person begins to increase his theta activity? We don't know of any such system in use at the present time, but we think it might work. A serious practical problem, however, is that most people don't like to be all wired up. Before any alertness-indicator type system would be accepted by pilots, air-traffic controllers, truck drivers and so on, it would have to be clearly demonstrated that such a system made an appreciable difference in performance.

O'Hanlon[6] has looked elsewhere in his continuing search for a physiological pattern which is indicative of alertness. In this case he was interested in driver fatigue, and the physiological measure that he looked at was heart rate variability, the degree to which your heart rate jumps around. The results of laboratory studies had suggested that as subjects became less alert, their heart rate variability increased. In order to test the relationship between driving performance, alertness, and heart rate variability, O'Hanlon hired three drivers each of whom drove over a 364-mile course in California in approximately eight hours on five consecutive days. They drove a converted van which had built into it equipment for recording heart rate and a place for an observer who noted driver errors; for example, lane drifts, unsafe passing, failure to signal, and tailgating.

The results of this real-world study showed that heart rate variability did, indeed, increase with driving time, as did driver errors. Interestingly, it was found that heart rate variability decreased sharply following two accidents. Rather than suggest that we have more car accidents in order to stay alert while driving, O'Hanlon has suggested the possibility of using heart rate variability as the long-sought physiological input to an alertness indicator.

The railroad industry has been experimenting with an alertness indicator which does not involve attaching any wires or electrodes to the engineer. An ultrasonic transmitter and sensing system has been designed which is sensitive to the motions of the engineer. A tone of a very high frequency (beyond that which you could hear) is bounced off of the engineer (he doesn't feel anything) and received by the sensor. In theory, the unalert or asleep engineer would be characterized by inactivity which would be sensed by the ultrasonic system. The system could then sound an alarm to awaken the engineer or, failing that, stop the train. This system has been installed and tested in a railroad cab but has been unsuccessful so far due to interference from vibrations of the cab.

We could give up trying to develop new biofeedback methods for dealing with the problem of alertness and use the old iron-spike-under-the-chin approach.

20

Lie Detection

Lie detection, as most people know, refers to a procedure whereby ANS (autonomic nervous system) measures such as GSR (galvanic skin response), blood pressure, and pulse rate are recorded from a person while being asked two types of questions: neutral questions and relevant questions. The relevant questions deal with specifics of the crime under investigation or details of some other aspect of the person's behavior.

For example, a government secret sleuthing agency desirous of hiring only redblooded all-American employees might well make use of a lie detector to ascertain whether or not you have ever engaged in any unusual sexual practices. Their concern is that you might be blackmailed into revealing secret information if your preference is for what is illegal in some places. Here, obviously, the relevant questions would deal with your sex life.

Neutral questions are always included in order to determine for each individual the magnitude of his ANS responses just to answering simple neutral questions. This varies greatly from person to person and without this information an individual might be falsely accused of being guilty just because he makes large ANS responses to all questions. Therefore, the measure of interest to the lie detector operator is the difference in the size of a person's ANS responses between neutral questions and relevant questions. If you didn't murder the girl in the red dress, a question about red dresses should bring about ANS responses from you no larger than your responses to neutral questions such as, is today Tuesday? However, if you are guilty, questions about red dresses will probably bring about ANS responses from you that are much larger than your responses to neutral questions.

There are two assumptions that we must make if we are to have faith in the validity of lie detection: (1) lying will cause heightened ANS responding, and (2) the ANS responses are not under voluntary control.

The first assumption is valid for most individuals. The second assumption is really what this book is all about. We have been saying over and over that with biofeedback, people can learn to control their ANS responses.

An interesting question that we[1] investigated in the following experiment was whether biofeedback in a lie detection situation would aid a suspect in controlling his responses and thereby confuse the interrogator, or if biofeedback would aid the interrogator in determining when the suspect was lying or telling the truth. The first possible outcome follows from the biofeedback work that we have reviewed. The second possible outcome was based on a hunch that we had. We felt that subjects who received biofeedback might make even larger than normal ANS responses when lying because they would receive immediate feedback which would indicate to them that they were revealing themselves to the interrogator.

In the real world, there are at least three ways that lie detector operators may inadvertently provide the person being interrogated with biofeedback. The most direct way would be if the person was permitted to feel his own pulse or other ANS responses. This could easily happen if the straps or tape that are used to secure the electrodes are too tight. Or the individual might perceive his own responses directly due to heightened emotional responding together with idiosyncratic sensitivity. A more indirect means of obtaining biofeedback would occur in cases where he or she could hear the movement of the polygraph galvonometers or pens. The most indirect source of biofeedback would occur if the interrogator looked at the polygraph record and then verbally or in some more subtle fashion revealed something about its contents. Should one try to provide the person being interrogated with biofeedback or should one try to eliminate all related cues? That is the practical question that we were investigating.

Three groups of subjects were studied in our experiment. One group received auditory feedback of their GSR while being interrogated. That is, their GSR was converted to a tone which changed in pitch with their changes in skin resistance. A second group received auditory feedback of their pulse rate. And a third group received no feedback at all. The subjects were 48 college students. After the subjects entered the experimental room, were seated, and listened to instructions that were tape recorded, GSR electrodes were attached. Note that the GSR was recorded from all three groups. If the subject had been assigned to a feedback group the appropriate device was attached and its output explained to the subject. The actual experiment had two phases. In the first phase we tried to determine which of five geometric figures the subject had selected and in the second phase we tried to determine which was the subject's social security number from among five sets of numbers.

The subjects were then interrogated individually concerning the five geometric figures. They were required to answer "No" as we asked them if each of the figures was the one they had selected. Next each subject was interrogated about the social security numbers.

Only the GSR data were used to determine detection. The results indicated that the subjects in the GSR feedback group were the easiest to detect. That is, the relative size of their GSRs to the critical stimulus (the one they selected) was greater than in the other groups. The pulse rate subjects were next easiest to detect. We also examined in this experiment whether it was easier to detect personal or nonpersonal stimuli. As you might guess, for all groups it was easier to detect personal stimuli—social security numbers.

In summary, those subjects who received auditory feedback of their GSR while being interrogated were significantly easier to detect than the control group which received no biofeedback. Would feedback of any ANS response yield the same results? No, the results indicate that the detectability of the group that received pulse rate feedback was not significantly different from that of the control group. Perhaps this was because GSR was the dependent variable—the actual measure of detection. If detectability had been measured in terms of pulse rate change, the results might have been quite different.

The results of this experiment support the second possible outcome that was mentioned above: Biofeedback aided the interrogators in determining when their subject was lying. What was the role of the biofeedback? We think that the biofeedback indicated to the subjects when they were starting to reveal themselves to the interrogator and this, in turn, caused additional ANS responding which helped the interrogator to detect when they were lying.

This appears to us to be related to a common finding in biofeedback research and therapy. Biofeedback is extremely useful in teaching people to make responses in the direction of increased arousal or activation but sometimes an actual hindrance when teaching people to relax. If a person is trying to reduce or keep constant his level of arousal, and he makes an increase, without biofeedback the increase might be very slight and short-lived. But with a biofeedback device saying "Error," the slight increase might become a large long-lasting increase in arousal.

What if we purposely gave the person the wrong feedback? False biofeedback refers to a deceptive laboratory procedure whereby subjects are told that they will be receiving biofeedback. For example, they may be told that they will hear their heart beating, but in fact, they hear a prerecorded tape recording of a beating noise.

The first ingenious false biofeedback experiment was conducted in the 1960s by Valins[2] with false heart rate feedback. Valins reasoned that since our emotional behavior is tied so closely to our ANS responding, we should be able to affect people's emotional behavior by presenting them with false biofeedback. To try out his idea, he presented ten slides of nude females to male subjects while they listened to what they thought was their own heart beat. The pre-recorded tape of the beating noise was so timed that while five of the slides were on the screen, their "heart beat" remained constant and while the other five were being exposed their "heart beat" dramatically increased. The subjects were then asked to rate the ten girls they had seen on the slides in terms of attractiveness. As you might have guessed, the girls who were on the screen when the subjects heard their "heart beat" increase were rated as significantly more attractive than those who were on the screen when the "heart beat" remained constant.

Pretty clever experiment, we thought and went on to think how we might apply the basic idea of false biofeedback to a lie detection situation.

The question we were asking when we began this experiment was whether false heart rate feedback—which was designed to make subjects believe that we could detect when they were lying and when they were telling the truth to a set of preliminary questions—would aid our detection during the actual interrogation which followed. Since, presumably, the difference in our bodily responses produced by truth-telling and lying is the result of prior conditioning (during early training way back in childhood), it was thought that further semantic conditioning in the laboratory, of the concepts of truth-telling and lying, would enhance the differences between such responses in subsequent interrogation.

We[3] were involved in a previous study along these lines in which lie responses during the semantic conditioning phase were followed by loud tones. The results of this study indicated that this preconditioning to truth-telling versus lying did, indeed, help to aid detection during the actual interrogation.

Since most people now agree that it is unethical to use highly aversive stimuli such as electric shock or very loud tones, we[4] designed a new study in which we used false biofeedback instead of such noxious stimuli during the preconditioning, or semantic conditioning, phase. We didn't use true biofeedback in this experiment. It was decided to use false feedback in this study since not all subjects could be relied upon to show noticeable changes in their heart rate when they lied during the preconditioning phase. It was thought that if the false heart beat was made to increase substantially following lies, the subjects would be led to assume that they were quite obviously revealing themselves to the interrogator whenever they lied during the preconditioning period and this would make them think twice before lying during the subsequent interrogation. And we went on to assume that such thinking twice would accentuate bodily responses to lies.

The GSR was used as the actual ANS measure of detection. Forty-five college students served as subjects. The procedure consisted of three phases: (1) the theft period, (2) the conditioning period, and (3) the interrogation period. During the theft period, the subject was led into the experimental room where he was left to read his instructions which requested him to commit a theft.

Confronted with three identical closed boxes, the subject was instructed to open just one of them, remove the object in it (a watch, key, or cigarette lighter) and conceal the object on his person. In addition, the subjects were asked to write the name of the object on a slip of paper and to conceal it also. This was done to insure that the subject actually did see the object in his chosen box.

During the conditioning phase 20 questions were presented, each on an individual slide. Subjects were instructed to answer the questions by pressing either a "yes" or a "no" button in front of them. They were told to lie on 5 of the 20 questions. For example, "Does it ever snow in Pennsylvania?" It was obvious to the subjects that they and the experimenter knew the true answer. GSR electrodes were attached to all subjects at the beginning of this phase. In addition, phony electrodes were attached and subjects were told that they would measure their pulse rate which would be amplified and played back for them over a speaker. At the start the false heart beat was set at 76 beats per minute, approximately normal. For one group of subjects, the experimental group, the rate was increased to 108 beats per minute following each of the five lies. The procedure was exactly the same for the control group except that they were told that the beats were just extraneous noises.

Immediately following the conditioning phase, the interrogation period began. In order to motivate the subjects, they were offered a bonus of $3 if they could successfully deceive the interrogator. Seven questions were then presented by slide and tape recorder simultaneously. A curious finding from the first few subjects run in this experiment was that in an attempt to deceive us, they simply closed their eyes and didn't read the questions that were being projected on the screen. That is why we started presenting the questions simultaneously by slide and tape recorder. Four of the questions were neutral and the other three concerned the objects that could have been taken. The false feedback was not used in this phase since only the subject knew for sure when he was lying.

The results of this study indicated that false heart rate feedback aided detection during the interrogation period. However, the difference in detectability between the experimental group and the control group was not great. Two possible explanations as to why we didn't get a greater difference in detectability are as follows. In the first place we used false *heart rate* feedback but we used *GSR* as our actual measure of detection. In the second place we used false heart rate feedback during the conditioning period but not during the actual interrogation period.

We recently described our false biofeedback lie detection procedure to a veteran police officer with many years' experience as a lie detector operator. We explained that the main reason for using the false feedback during the period immediately prior to the interrogation was to convince the suspect that we could tell when he was lying. The police officer smiled and replied that even though (until our conversation) he had never heard of biofeedback, he had been using a similar procedure successfully for years. He then described how he dealt with a suspect just before starting to formally question him about the crime. He would quite informally ask unimportant questions not related to the crime until he thought the suspect had lied. At this point he would frown at the suspect and slap his nightstick against his hand. His purpose was the same as ours: to convince the suspect that he could tell when he had lied and in so doing to enhance the magnitude of the suspect's physiological responses to any lies told during the actual interrogation. We think that there is a future for false biofeedback in lie detection. And, going back to the first experiment described in this chapter, we feel that a lie detection procedure making use of true biofeedback is ready to be tried in a real-life (out of the laboratory) situation.

21

Creativity and the Human Potential

> Does anyone have a map? A map of what? A map of where we are going. Oh. Do you know where we are going? No. But I can tell when we get there. How will you know? By the map. Who drew the map? Those who imagined what it will be like when we get there. Oh.
>
> They don't really know what it is like either. No, they just guess. But, some are better guessers than others. The good guessers, what are they called? Inventors, pioneers, Einsteins. Could we get there without a map? Yes, but we wouldn't know we were there. Oh.

Concerning our body and health, we are very much like individuals without maps. We just constantly drive on. We have some sense when we are lost or off our course, which is commonly called being sick. We have even set up the equivalent of the road service branch of the AAA with our elaborate medical complexes and systems. This is not to claim that medical facilities are bad, rather they are very good. But it is also clear to anyone walking into one of these facilities that disease and pathology have established themselves as the dictators of these institutions. Without a doubt, the "medical problems" that a person faces have been translated into a micro-level behavioral environment and separated from the person. It is a cliche but true that many doctors now treat diseases and not individuals.

The outcome of this emphasis on pathology has led some individuals both within and without the medical profession to suggest that we have misplaced our emphasis and that it is now time to return to the treatment of the whole person. We now see a return to family practice. Groups are being organized which use such terms as holistic medicine, humanistic psychology, and so forth. Major universities are now offering symposia on both ancient and modern methods of healing that retain the integrity of the human being. We also see a new emphasis being placed on the two processes that we all encounter as human beings, those of birth

and death. In a sense there is a movement for a reintegration of the individual with himself in all facets of his life.

Out of this movement is coming a new stress on health and growth. The new emphasis no longer sees health as just the absence of disease but as a separate process that is worthy of development. Biofeedback with its emphasis on the person listening to himself and accepting his processing as his own has been incorporated into and seen as a tool of the new holistic medicine movement. At present, there is mainly speculation as to how biofeedback can be utilized in the development of man's potential. Some of this speculation will appear crazy and most likely will be left behind as the field moves on. Other speculation will become the ground work for what might become a reorganization or evolution of our present medical and psychological treatment system. In this chapter we want to look at some of the work that is going on and speculations that are being made. In essence, biofeedback as directed toward the discovery of human potential is really an invitation to imagination. It is that same imagination that sent Columbus looking for India and Einstein riding on a beam of light. Neither really accomplished what they set out to do, but the world is a different place because of both of their journeys.

Abraham Maslow has written a great deal in terms of humanistic psychology and was influential in both the founding of the Association of Humanistic Psychology and the Association for Transpersonal Psychology.[1] He suggested an important approach to the study of human potential. In addition to our study of the disease process, Maslow thought we should also direct our attention in the other direction, toward what he called the "good specimen." The "good specimen" for Maslow is the man or woman who is living more within their potential, the person who lives his or her life to the fullest. In the East these people are called masters and in the West, great leaders of one form or another. Maslow's point is that in psychology and medicine we spend most of our time discussing pathology and hardly talk about how life could be at its best.

One study which aimed at examining the "good specimen" was carried out in Joe Kamiya's laboratory in San Francisco. In this study, Zen meditators who were considered masters were asked to meditate while psychophysiological recordings, especially EEG (brain wave activity) were made. In a further analysis of the data reported recently by Jim Hardt,[2] it was revealed that not only did one see differences in the EEG meditation patterns of beginning and advanced meditators, but further there were differences in the order in which the beginner and advanced meditator produced alpha and theta waves. For example, Dr. Hardt found that there were not only periods of alpha activity which were seen to move throughout the brain of advanced meditators as meditation continued but also there were periods of predominant theta activity which were not found in the beginning meditators. Through some very sophisticated mathematical analyses these researchers were also able to show that during the meditations of the advanced meditators there were periods in which both sides of the brain were functioning in synchrony. Literally being of one mind. Can producing the same EEG activity from both of your hemispheres make you of one mind? No one knows but it is an intriguing thought.

Recent research has demonstrated that the hemispheres of our brain process information differently from one another.[3] The general formulation is that the left hemisphere deals with information in a linear, temporal, "scientific," and verbal manner, whereas the right hemisphere tends to process information holistically or in terms of relationships and the total gestalt. That is, the right hemisphere does not describe or break-up information but rather processes the "big picture" or the totality of the situation. Consider how reading a description about the inside of someone's home and walking through their house yourself will affect your memory and picture of their house, and you can see some of the difference between learning with each hemisphere.

David Galin pointed out certain similarities between characteristics of right hemispheric functioning and what Freud and the later analysts referred to as primary process, a nontemporal, nonverbal mode of expression of psychic components.[4] Dr. Galin further suggests that one basis of what we call psychological conflict may be the result of the two hemispheres acting without regard for one another. For example, consider the situation in which a small child hears (with the left hemisphere) his or her mother say "I really love you and I am only doing this for your own good" while at the same time he sees (with the right hemisphere) the mother's expression being that of tension and anger. It is clear that in this case the child's memories of his mommy would be very different depending upon the hemisphere involved and thus create for the person an underlying level of conflict. Biofeedback might lead to a method of exploring and reintegrating the two hemispheres in the above case. But first we must ask if individuals can learn to control one hemisphere relative to the other through biofeedback.

In our own laboratory we have found that individuals can learn to control the relationship of the electrical output between the two hemispheres.[5] Subjects were set in front of a television-like screen on which a line graph was being drawn. The position of the line graph was determined by the average EEG power of one hemisphere compared to the other. With this type of feedback most of the individuals were successful in moving the graph to one side of the screen or the other when instructed. The graph was moved by changing the power ratio output of one hemisphere of the brain in relation to the other. What does this mean? Of course we don't know for sure. It does suggest that we have much more control over our physiology than we ever suspected. Also this may have implications for our understanding of emotional processes since one of our subjects reported that he did not like moving the graph in the direction that demonstrated right hemisphere functioning, since when he did so he had thoughts of love and art and these thoughts troubled him.

Whether the cola people were literally correct when they claimed that it is the *pause* that refreshes is uncertain. Yet we face a similar question when evaluating the effects of alpha training. As some of the popular ads would have us believe, alpha training is said to help you to sell more real estate, to play better golf, and even to have better sex. About these activities and alpha we don't know and probably, because of all the misinformation around, we will never be able to find out. However, there is considerable evidence to suggest that the subjective state that accompanies alpha activity is one of well being and relaxation. This has sent a number of people around the country talking about alpha as a replacement for drugs. There have also been reports of creative individuals being better able to control their alpha than individuals who are not as creative. In the long run it may turn out that alpha training itself is a valuable technique, not so much for the ability to turn alpha off and on but for the new relationship with your body that must be established. First you must learn to listen and to feel what is going on within your body without wanting to change it or make it different. And second, you have to adopt a passive attitude toward the desire to produce alpha and just allow alpha activity to come forth. For the general population to have learned these two techniques alone may, for the human potential movement, have been worth all the fuss and craziness over alpha.

Whereas alpha caught the imagination of the popular press, theta caught the imagination of the biofeedback researchers.[6] Theta activity is the low frequency activity that has been associated with drowsiness and hypnagogic imagery. Hypnagogic imagery is that dreamlike state that you may experience just as you are about to fall asleep. You are not really awake and not not really asleep and your mind becomes like a movie in which you pleasantly watch the scenes go by.

Why would you want to increase theta activity if it is only associated with sleep? The answer is simple. Because it will enrich your life. The reasoning is that since theta activity is associated with dreamlike states of imagery, or what has been called reverie, and since these states of reverie have been seen by various creative people as the ground from which their creative ideas sprang, then training in theta should also lead to greater creativity and enrichment of life. Drs. Green, Green, and Walters at the Menninger Foundation in Topeka have performed research since the late 1960s relating theta training and creativity.[7] Their preliminary results do suggest that within theta activity lies one key for releasing new energy for personal development. From their work it appears as if theta activity is associated with entry into that area of our psyche that we call the unconscious, that is, childhood memories, dreams, and archetypal images such as gods, teachers, and so forth. For those individuals ready for a journey inward, biofeedback may prove to be useful as an objective external record of the internal states explored. Whether or not through biofeedback we might satisfy the dream of Carl Jung and find the psychic counterpart of nuclear energy and thus make available a new source of power for human development is unknown. However, the possibility seems well worth the search.

Although technology and especially biofeedback technology may offer us new avenues for exploring man's potential, we must always remember how we fit into the process. Our history is one of misplaced emphasis upon the potential of the technique more than the potential of ourselves. If we are going to escape this trap with biofeedback, man must rightly be seen as the instrument of his own evolution. In the process, he may choose other instrumental methods for helping him achieve his goal of living out his potential. But from these, too, he must liberate himself if he is to continue exploring ever new areas of his own being.

part four

Biofeedback: Problems and Promises

22

Summing Up

Summarizing what has been done in the field of biofeedback has been relatively easy, evaluating what has been done is extremely difficult. We will do our best to assess, in our opinions, the current state of biofeedback, but we do want you to keep in mind that we are trying to evaluate something very new and ongoing.

We would say in summary that *biofeedback therapy is bringing about improvement in the condition of numerous patients with a variety of problems, some of whom have not been helped by any other type of therapy.*

Let us turn to some of the specific problems that make it so difficult for us to give you a more definitive assessment of biofeedback. In the first place it is hard to evaluate the clinical effectiveness of biofeedback in laboratory situations where the experimenter is concerned with group behavior. To quote from Erik Peper[1] "... biofeedback learning is not group behavior but learning unique to an individual. The term 'statistical average' in biofeedback training is as meaningless as the term 'normal person' in clinical assessment."

Laboratory studies give us certain kinds of information about biofeedback, but laboratory studies cannot tell us whether a certain type of biofeedback therapy will be better for patient X than another type of biofeedback therapy or some entirely different type of therapy, because of the large number of individual factors such as the motivation of the patient, the personality of the therapist, the nature of the biofeedback, and many others, all of which seem to be important. There are so many factors involved in successful biofeedback treatment that at this time it is hard to make predictions about the effectiveness of the therapy for a particular individual based on group data.

We said in our summary statement above that people are getting better following biofeedback therapy. However, we want to call to your attention again something that we mentioned in an earlier chapter. That is, a great deal goes into the total situation that we are calling biofeedback therapy. And what we really don't know at this time is, are the people getting better from the biofeedback per se? To put this another way, is biofeedback the active ingredient in some of the cures that are being reported following the use of biofeedback therapy? We don't really know.

Another problem that arises when we try to assess biofeedback is that many people confuse significant laboratory results with clinically significant results. These are two different concepts.

In laboratory studies a particular biofeedback procedure is often compared with some other procedure. Let's take, for example, a study comparing the effectiveness of biofeedback and TM (trancendental meditation) for lowering one's heart rate. We might well find that the biofeedback group lowered its heart rate an average of four beats per minute and the TM group two beats. A statistical test might yield a significant difference, but this says nothing about whether such a difference is clinically significant. On the other hand, if we were working with hospitalized patients who had to lower their heart rates approximately 30 beats per minute in order to avoid serious medical problems, the result brought about by biofeedback therapy in the hypothetical laboratory experiment described above would not be considered clinically significant. An average change of 4 beats might be statistically significant when compared with a change of 2 beats per minute, but if your patient requires a change of 30 beats or more to live, the procedure which brought about the 4-beat change is of little value.

Getting the patient off the machine is another problem in both biofeedback research and therapy. In order for biofeedback to be a realistic type of therapy, it must be possible at some point to take off the electrodes and detach the patient from the biofeedback apparatus. We feel that some researchers and some therapists have failed to come to grips with this issue. Previous work, discussed in other chapters, has shown that it is sometimes possible to wean the patient from the biofeedback equipment and still maintain the desired effect. Basmajian's work with EMG (recording electrical activity of a muscle from the skin) biofeedback for foot drop is an example. In other cases such as biofeedback treatment for nocturnal bruxism, it has been found that when the biofeedback is withheld, the teeth grinding starts all over again.

We see here another difference between the goals of a laboratory researcher and a biofeedback therapist, someone actually working with patients. The laboratory worker may be interested in demonstrating that a certain type of biofeedback brings about a certain effect. The nocturnal bruxism studies are an example. The researchers applied the biofeedback and noted the effect, then took away the biofeedback and noted the return to prebiofeedback behavior. The laboratory researcher may be very pleased with these results because he has learned that biofeedback brings about a certain effect. Very interesting for the researcher but, in most cases, little help for the therapist and his patient.

Ideally, of course, what we hope to do for patients is to provide them with biofeedback and have this enable them to become aware of new sensitivities to their own internal bodily changes. If they succeed when the biofeedback is withheld they will be able to make use of new sensitivities to their own internal changes to maintain the desired bodily changes.

Another problem in assessing the effects of biofeedback is a problem that we have in evaluating any type of therapy. That is, are the effects lasting? What are the results of follow-up investigations of the patients? If you came to us for help with your migraine headaches, we would with the aid of biofeedback teach you over the course of approximately ten sessions to warm your hands and cool your head. By the tenth session you might report that you are no longer having headaches. But what is the state of your head after three months? And after a year?

Some types of therapy are only effective as long as the patient is seeing the therapist. Others last a little longer and those that are truly successful last a lifetime. Since biofeedback as a form of therapy is relatively new, it is particularly difficult for us to gather follow-up data describing the condition of individuals who have been treated with biofeedback for gastrointestinal disorders, high blood pressure, bruxism, and so forth. But such information is really essential before we can completely evaluate biofeedback therapy.

The last problem that we will mention is the matter of the expense for the equipment and the specialized training for the therapist. The average price for a single piece of biofeedback equipment designed to record and display one physiological measure is approximately $300. The specialized training that a therapist should receive, in our opinion, would require taking courses in biofeedback and in psychophysiology, of which biofeedback is only a small specialization.

We are not suggesting that anyone could become a competent biofeedback therapist by taking a couple of courses and buying a piece of equipment. We are saying that a professional therapist such as a clinical psychologist, a physical therapist, or a physician could start using biofeedback as an adjunct to their usual therapy following appropriate training. And to you who would like to receive biofeedback therapy for some disorder, we suggest that you seek out the help of a traditional practitioner who uses biofeedback as an adjunct to his usual variety of therapies. For example, if your heart is missing beats, find a cardiologist who has been trained in biofeedback in addition to his other medical skills. Or find a cardiologist who is working with another professional, perhaps a psychologist who is a trained biofeedback therapist. If you have severe headaches, go to a neurologist and after he diagnoses you as having migraine headaches, as opposed to a brain tumor, ask him if he knows of someone who could give you biofeedback therapy.

Why request biofeedback therapy? The simplest answer we would give would be to quote ourselves: Biofeedback is bringing about improvement in the condition of numerous patients with a variety of problems, some of whom have not been helped by any other type of therapy.

What are some other reasons why we are working with and writing about biofeedback even though there are many problems and unanswered questions?

We think that one of the most attractive aspects of biofeedback therapy is that with biofeedback the responsibility for changing your condition is left up to you. You must practice bringing about the desired bodily change until you can do it without biofeedback. The therapist cannot do it for you. We think that this is the way it should be and many patients with whom we have spoken have embraced this notion.

Another aspect of biofeedback that appeals to us is that with biofeedback people get to know their bodies better than they ever did before. Here, we are talking about a uniting of mind and body that is absent in most Western thought but is, of course, one of the major concepts of most Eastern philosophies.

Reducing the use of drugs is another feature of biofeedback as far as we are concerned. A woman came to us recently requesting help for her migraine headaches. She had been suffering from them for about ten years and had been to several physicians and a neurologist. They gave her drugs to ease the pain, drugs to decrease the amount of blood in the extracranial arteries of the head, drugs to tranquilize her and still she was having on the average one to two headaches per *day* when she came to see us. We provided her with some biofeedback equipment and instruction so that she could learn to control the temperature of her hands and head and we introduced her to some autogenic training phrases to aid her in learning to control her skin temperature. She recently called us to say that she had gone an entire week without a headache and without taking any medication. Prior to treatment she was taking capsules and suppositories once or twice a day and sometimes more often.

Some might say yes, we helped this woman, but just substituted biofeedback and autogenic training for another therapy, namely, drugs. Indeed, we have and we think that there are two very good reasons for being pleased with this substitution—in addition to the fact that the incidence of her headaches has been drastically reduced. In the first place most drugs powerful enough to bring about a specific desired bodily change will also bring about undesirable side effects. An obvious example is a painkiller that makes you so groggy that you can't work, drive, or perhaps even think. And we have never heard of a person dying of an overdose of biofeedback.

The second undesirable effect of most drugs is that they interfere with the normally-occurring feedback systems within the body. Drugs prevent you from getting to know your body. Put more technically, drugs prevent the occurrence of normal healthy feedback between your brain and other parts of your body which are innervated by the autonomic nervous system. For example, if you make a habit of gobbling up a 16-inch pepperoni pizza, running off to a meeting, suffering from pains in the abdomen, and taking various drugs to relieve your distress you are not only failing to get to know your body, to communicate with it, you are probably confusing the hell out of it. Your brain received a signal from your stomach, pain, which should have been a sufficient message for you to stop eating pizzas on the run. Instead, you have tried to muffle the message with drugs rather than dealing with the behavior that leads to the distress. This may work for a while, but you have probably noticed that the messages are getting louder and louder. Even though a drug may temporarily muffle the message the cumulative wear and tear on the body will take its eventual toll.

Our migraine headache patient used to respond to her messages, the first signs of pains in her head, with various powerful drugs. They would give some immediate but temporary relief and the messages kept getting louder. Now, instead of interfering with her body's normal feedback systems by taking drugs, when she feels the first signs of a headache coming on she gets the message and wherever she is—at home, at work, in her car—she stops what she is doing and does her biofeedback-autogenic training exercises. In most cases she is successful in aborting her headaches.

In conclusion, in terms of what has been done with biofeedback during the past ten years we would say that the greatest gains or improvements have been made when biofeedback has been used with responses controlled by the central nervous system, that is, muscle potential changes and brain wave activity. There have been some definite beneficial effects when biofeedback has been used with some responses controlled by the autonomic nervous system, but, in general, the autonomically controlled changes have not been as great. We think that this difference in magnitude of bodily change between CNS (central nervous system) and ANS (autonomic nervous system) responses is as one would expect. We have been controlling voluntarily our muscles and, in a way of speaking, our brain all of our lives, but most of us have left our heart, lungs, and stomach to their own devices. If it takes many months to learn to use the muscles of our fingers to play the piano we should not expect to learn to play our internal organs in five easy lessons.

We do not want to leave you with the idea that biofeedback is the answer to all medical and psychological problems. In fact, it is difficult at this time to say exactly with which disorders biofeedback will prove to be the most useful. What we can suggest is that you seek to be an enlightened consumer—that you examine some of the current evaluations of biofeedback therapy in either books[2] or journals[3] and that you talk with professionals before you engage in any treatment program. It should be pointed out that evaluating a treatment such as biofeedback is not as easy as it sounds and that it takes more than enthusiasm and testimonials to prove a treatment successful.

Ray, Raczynski, Rogers, and Kimball[2] suggest that at least three separate questions must be asked in the evaluation of clinical biofeedback. First, is there scientific evidence to demonstrate that the treatment is effective? This is a very complex question since many new treatments ranging from medication to meditation seem to work when they are first introduced only to be shown later to be ineffective. Second, is it an acceptable alternative to current clinical treatments? That is, you may choose biofeedback over surgery if equally effective since biofeedback is more economical and does not result in irreversible changes to the body. Third, does it help the person to think and act in more healthy ways? That is to say, biofeedback itself may not directly produce a "cure" but may lead people to a new understanding of their problems which in turn leads to improvement.

In many cases this new understanding has led the person to take a more active role in treating his or her own problems, as was the case of the woman with headaches discussed previously. For people like her, biofeedback may represent the first step in reestablishing a link with their bodies, for example, learning to relax in the middle of stress, learning when to say no to certain types of foods, and learning when to seek professional help. Most people do not need biofeedback to stop and listen to their bodies, but for people who are hard of hearing, it may be the essential first step.

Although new clinical and research reports concerning biofeedback are appearing daily, the final evaluation of the technique remains far in the future. We have attempted in this book, not to evaluate biofeedback, but to show you how it has been used and to suggest how it might be used in the future. Biofeedback is one way in which some individuals have sought to increase the communications they receive from their body, and through this communication, actively to seek health and well-being. It is by no means the only way.

part five
Biofeedback: More Information

23
Sources of Additional Information

I. Associations

    The Biofeedback Research Society
        Francine Butler, Executive Secretary
        University of Colorado Medical Center
        4200 East Ninth Avenue
        Denver, Colorado 80220

    American Association of Biofeedback Clinicians
        Jeanine Gavin
        Incentives
        Des Plaines, Illinois 60016

II. Journals

    Biofeedback and Self-Regulation, the new journal of The Biofeedback Research Society.

    Psychophysiology, the journal of the Society for Psychophysiological Research sometimes contains articles about biofeedback.

    Psychosomatic Medicine, articles about psychological and physiological interrelationships and sometimes biofeedback.

III. Books

    Birk, L. (Ed.). *Biofeedback: Behavioral Medicine.* New York: Grune & Stratton, 1973.

Brown, B. B. *New Mind, New Body.* New York: Harper, 1974.

Brown, B. B. (Ed.). *The Biofeedback Syllabus.* Springfield, Ill.: Thomas, 1975.

Butler, F., & Stoyva, J. (Eds.). *Biofeedback and Self-Regulation, A Bibliography.* Denver: Biofeedback Research Society, 1973.

Jonas, G. *Visceral Learning.* New York: Viking, 1972.

Karlins, M., & Andrews, L. *Biofeedback: Turning on the Power of Your Mind.* New York: Lippincott, 1972.

McCrady, R. E., & McCrady, J. B. *Biofeedback: An Annotated Bibliography of Published Research with Human Subjects Since 1960.* Pomona, Calif.: Behavioral Instrument Co., 1975.

Owen, S.; Toomim, H.; & Taylor, L. P. *Biofeedback in Neuromuscular Re-Education.* Los Angeles: Biofeedback Research Institute, 1975.

Stern, R. M., & Ray, W. J. *Biofeedback and the Control of Internal Bodily Activity.* Homewood, Ill.: Learning Systems, 1975.

IV. Annuals

Every year since 1970, Aldine Publishing Co. has brought out a volume entitled *Biofeedback and Self-Control* edited by T. X. Barber, L. V. DiCara, J. Kamiya, N. E. Miller, D. Shapiro and J. Stoyva. (The order of the listing of editors changes each year.) Each issue contains reprints of articles dealing with biofeedback that have appeared during the past year in various journals. In 1970 the same company published the *Biofeedback Reader* which contains reprints of older articles which are relevant to biofeedback.

V. Cassette Tapes

A number of tapes dealing with applications of biofeedback are available from BioMonitoring Applications, 270 Madison Ave., New York, New York 10016.

A tape, *Facts and Fancy about Biofeedback and Its Clinical Implications,* by Neal Miller, presented at the 1973 meeting of the American Psychological Association is available.

Two tapes, *Biofeedback and Self-Control,* recorded at a panel discussion at the 1976 meeting of the American Association for the Advancement of Science are available.

VI. Films and Video Tapes

Biofeedback: Program 2 of *The Behavioral Revolution*, 1975, 30 minute color videocassette. Available from: The Pennsylvania State University. Audio-Visual Services, 7 Willard Building, University Park, PA 16802. *The Behavioral Revolution* is a five-part series that explores the history of psychology and the development of behaviorist theory, the varied application of behavioral technology, the specialized field of biofeedback, and the ethical questions that surround the applications of behavioral technology.

Biofeedback: Listening to Your Head, 1973, 22 min., color. Available from: Ideal Pictures, Inc., 321 W. 44th St., New York, NY 10036. Neurophysiologist Dr. Barbara Brown and biomusician David Rosenbloom introduce concepts which many scientists believe will eventually enable man to control his body and mind. Produced by Document Associates. From the Towards the Year 2000 series.

Involuntary Control, 1971, 20 min., color. Available from John Wiley and Sons, Inc., 605 Third Avenue, New York, NY 10016. Research on organism's control of its involuntary behavior. Laboratory experiments train rats to alter their heart rate and humans to emit alpha waves. Illustrates technique of shaping, the process of operant conditioning of autonomic responses, and technology of physiological psychology. Consultant: Dr. Neal Miller.

Mind Over Body, 1972, 49 min., color. Available from: Time-Life Broadcast, Inc., Time and Life Building, Rockefeller Center, 1271 Avenue of the Americas, New York, NY 10020. Routine illnesses and bodily injuries are greatly influenced by psychological state of patient. Interviews with doctors and psychologists conducting research are alternated with sequences of experiments in progress. Control of involuntary bodily functions: heartbeat, flow of blood, brain waves. Produced by BBC.

The Mind of Man: Parts 1-4, 1970, 27 min. each, color. Available from: Indiana University, Audio-Visual Center, Bloomington, IN 47401. Recent research on mental development in children; effects of drugs; dreams; brain structure; chemical changes within the brain; the brain and sexuality; reasoning; how the mind controls body functions. Interviews with Richard Fineman, Sir John Eccles, Noam Chomsky, Donald Hebb, Neil Miller, B. F. Skinner. Produced by NET.

24

The Instruments Used to Do Biofeedback

By now you realize that electronic equipment is involved in most biofeedback work. We say "most" because we happen to believe that successful biofeedback therapy can sometimes be accomplished by a clever therapist and a highly motivated patient without any electronic gadgets. For example, a common procedure that is currently being used to help migraine headache patients (details in Chapter 11) is to have them warm their hands and cool their heads. In a clinic or laboratory, the patient's hand and head temperature is usually recorded with the aid of an expensive skin temperature biofeedback device, and feedback to the subject is in terms of a meter display which depicts the difference between the head and hand temperature. The patient's job is to reduce that difference. We have found that migraine patients can conduct a simple exercise at home without expensive skin temperature biofeedback instruments. They touch their fingers to their temple and relax until they no longer feel any difference in temperature between their head and their hand.

Granted that electronic instruments can give more exact biofeedback information which is essential in some cases and that information about the functioning of some of our bodily changes is nonexistent without electronic devices, for example, the rate at which your stomach is contracting. What follows is an attempt to provide you with an introduction to biofeedback instruments.[1]

Biofeedback instruments are really special cases of more general equipment which is used in hospitals, clinics, doctors' offices, and research laboratories for the recording of bodily responses.[2] What is special about biofeedback instruments is that they are always equipped to let the patient know how he is responding. For example, your doctor uses his stethoscope to listen to your heart for diagnostic purposes. He does not usually let you listen in. However, if he wanted to use his stethoscope as a biofeedback device to try to help you control your heart rate, he might simply add an amplifier and a speaker to his equipment. Now you could both listen! Before biofeedback equipment was commercially available, we used the standard physiological recording equipment in our laboratory and just added a meter so that the subject could see his responses—or a tone so that he could hear his bodily changes.

What are the basic components of a biofeedback instrument?

Basic Components of a Biofeedback Instrument

Sensing Device	Signal Conditioner	Amplifier	Feedback Display and Permanent Record

The Sensing Device

The bare bones of a biofeedback instrument are shown in the accompanying table. A sensing device can refer to electrodes or transducers. Electrodes are small metal discs which are applied to the skin and usually used in pairs to record one physiological measure such as heart rate. They pick up the bioelectric signal from the body and wires attached to them carry the tiny electrical signal to a signal conditioner. Good quality electrodes are commonly made out of silver and are specially treated by the manufacturer so that they may be used over and over. They are technically referred to as silver-silver chloride electrodes. Before the electrodes are attached, the skin is lightly abraded to remove the dead cells on the surface which would interfere with good electrode contact. Actual attachment is usually done with tape. Electrode jelly (a mixture of salt and some jelly-like substance such as glycerin) is placed on the electrode before it is applied to the skin, again, to insure good electrode contact.

Why all this talk about good electrode contact? Two reasons.

First of all, if we don't have good electrode contact[3] we will miss part of the signal we are trying to record, brain waves, for example. And in the second place, we will record unwanted signals, artifacts, from sources such as the electrical interference generated by nearby electric motors.

Electrodes are commonly used to record EEG, EMG, GSRs, heart rate, and eye movements. Transducers are used to measure respiration, pulse volume, and skin temperature.

Transducers convert a physical change into a corresponding electrical output. To record respiration, we attach a thin rubber tube filled with mercury around the subject's chest. A small current is passed through the tube and a wire is inserted in each end and from there goes to the signal conditioner. When the subject inhales and his chest gets larger, he stretches the tube thinner which converts to an increase in resistance and hence a corresponding electrical output. This type of transducer is referred to as a strain gage.

We use a photocell transducer to record pulse volume[4] in the fingers. The actual device that fits on the finger contains a very small light bulb and a photocell, such as is used in photographic light meters. The light shines at the finger and depending upon the amount of blood in the finger, which depends upon how relaxed or tense you are, more or less light is reflected back down into the photocell. The photocell then converts an amount of light into a change in resistance and we, again, have a corresponding electrical output.

The final type of transducer we will talk about is used to measure skin temperature. Here we use what looks like a fat electrode. We tape it to the skin in the area of interest. It is either a thermistor or thermocouple. The former changes in resistance with temperature and the latter changes in voltage with the temperature. Most biofeedback skin temperature instruments make use of thermistors, but with either type of device we are converting changes in temperature to a corresponding electrical output.

Signal Conditioners

Signal conditioners, the second major functional component in a biofeedback instrument, usually contain preamplifiers and filters.

Preamplifiers are necessary because the electrical signals picked up from the body by electrodes and the output of most transducers are very small, in the microvolt or millivolt range. Preamplifiers commonly increase the size of the signal 500, or even 1,000 times. Filters are used to select only those signals with the frequency of interest and to block out interfering signals. For example, if you have a high quality EEG alpha biofeedback instrument, it probably contains filters that allow signals in the alpha range to pass, 8-13 Hz., but block out other EEG frequencies and block 60 Hz. electrical interference.

The main or power amplifiers increase the filtered signal to the point where it is strong enough to bring about observable changes on a meter, an oscilloscope, a tape recorder, an ink-writing recorder, a computer or some other type of display and/or recording device.

There are approximately 40 companies selling over 175 different biofeedback devices. The products they sell range in price from about $25 to $2,000 for a single piece of equipment. The most readily available instruments include the following: EEG, EMG, skin temperature, and galvanic skin response devices.

What to Consider in Buying Equipment

As of now there are no accepted standards in the biofeedback equipment industry, therefore, as you can imagine, there are some instruments being sold that don't do what their manufacturers claim they do. If you are considering buying biofeedback equipment or if you just want a better understanding as to what it is and what it does, here are some general considerations concerning biofeedback instruments.

Safety. The first consideration is safety. Unless you are technically capable of determining whether a person attached to the equipment could receive a painful or even fatal electric shock, it is best to use battery operated biofeedback devices. Depending upon the design of the equipment the batteries may last from a few hours to several hundred hours, another consideration because of cost and convenience.

Size. Another obvious difference between different instruments is physical size. Here you have to think of practical matters such as where the equipment will be used and to what extent it will be moved about.

Amount of Use. Another consideration is how well the unit will hold up to hard use. Will it frequently need adjustment or repair? Where do you send it to be repaired? How long is the delay? And what is the cost for common repairs? Answers to these service questions can best be obtained from people who are now using the equipment you are thinking of buying. A reputable manufacturer will on request send you a list of users of the instrument.

Electrodes. The electrodes supplied with the biofeedback instrument are very important. Without good quality electrodes, it doesn't matter how good the rest of the system is, you will not be happy with the results. One of the first considerations should be, are the electrodes replaceable? That is, can you conveniently remove the old electrodes and plug in new ones when necessary? Ideally, the biofeedback unit should come with a jack or connector into which you plug the electrodes. We are amazed at the number of biofeedback instruments that come with the electrodes permanently attached so that when the electrodes deteriorate, as they all do with use, the unit is nonfunctional. A person with some electronic skill can usually open up the instrument, cut the old electrode wires, and solder in new electrodes. But this shouldn't be necessary. In general, there is not enough emphasis on good quality electrodes, skin preparation, and proper attachment of the electrodes by equipment manufacturers.

Measure. One of the most basic considerations concerning any biofeedback instrument is—does it really measure what it claims to measure? We have seen some inexpensive EEG biofeedback equipment that rather than sounding a tone whenever alpha was present, sounded its tone whenever electrical interference was present. This question of the validity of the instrument is a difficult one for an individual who has not worked in electrical engineering, psychophysiology, or a related field. We would suggest that when in doubt, consult with an engineer or psychophysiologist at a nearby university or large hospital.

Sensitivity. Another consideration that is very basic is the sensitivity of the instrument. We are using "sensitivity" here to refer to the ability of the unit to pick up and feed back to the subject very small changes in whatever physiological response you are recording. If you are interested in training people to lower their muscle potential from five to two microvolts, you had better make sure that the equipment you are thinking of using is capable of discriminating such small changes in muscle potentials.

Range. The range of the equipment is also very important. When we talk about "range," we are getting into the issue of individual differences in subjects' physiological responses. An equipment manufacturer may find it cheaper to design the electronic circuit for his galvanic skin response biofeedback unit so that it can deal with individuals whose responses fall between 10,000 and 100,000 ohms. This will probably work fine for 90 percent of your subjects. But what about the other 10 percent? Their skin resistance falls either below 10,000 or above 100,000 ohms and with this equipment you will not be able to record from them. Or if you are working with pulse rate and your equipment is designed to go up to 100 pulses per minute and you get a patient with a pulse of 150, you are out of business.

Unwanted Signals. The next consideration is the ability of the equipment to block unwanted signals. Unwanted signals come in two varieties. Unwanted external signals include stray radio signals and 60 Hz. electrical interference from the electrical power lines. Unwanted internal signals include all of the bioelectronic signals being produced by your subject's body except the one you are trying to work with. Various filtering methods are used in different biofeedback instruments and the extent to which they do their job is crucial to your getting appropriate biofeedback.

Number of Locations. The number of channels, or the number of locations from which you can record simultaneously, is a consideration. If you are doing skin temperature recording from a migraine patient, for example, you might want to record simultaneously hand temperature and head temperature and have the flexibility in your instrument of feeding back to the patient one or the other or the difference between them. If you are doing muscle potential recording from a person suffering from an imbalance such as torticollis, the head being bent to one side, you might want to record simultaneously from the appropriate muscle on the left and on the right side and present dual feedback to help the individual lessen the muscle activity on the overactive side and strengthen the activity on the weak side.

Permanent Record. The next item that we want to mention is the advantage of being able to record permanently the output of your instrument. More expensive units usually come with a jack or connector which provides this output which may be used with a tape recorder, ink-writer recorder, and so forth. This is very important for purposes of keeping track of progress across sessions, whether you are doing therapy or research.

Output. Another consideration is also related to output. This time we are talking about the importance of your being aware of the output, of what is currently being recorded from the subject, at all times, even when you don't want the subject to receive biofeedback for one reason or another. Again, this is often done on better quality equipment by having appropriately labeled output jacks. This feature is important because there will be times such as when your subject is well on his way to learning how to control the particular physiological response you have been working with when you want to wean him off of biofeedback. But it is still essential that *you* be able to monitor his responding.

Mode of Feedback. The next consideration is the mode of feedback. What is the nature of the biofeedback that will be provided to your subject? With some equipment this is auditory, with others it is visual. With some instruments it is continuous, with others it is discrete. You would like the most flexible biofeedback possible. There are times when visual feedback, for example, is inappropriate such as when you are doing something which requires the subject to keep his eyes closed or in cases where visual attention will interfere with the response under study.

Shaping. We think that one of the most important aspects of biofeedback equipment is that it be so designed to make "shaping" of the subject's response possible. "Shaping," a term we have used previously, is sometimes referred to as the method of successive approximations in operant conditioning. During the first few sessions, it should be possible to reward the subject with biofeedback for very small changes which are in the correct direction. As the sessions progress, we would want to demand more and more in terms of changes in the desired direction before the subject would receive rewarding biofeedback. Ideally, there should be some way of presetting a criterion for a "correct response" for a given session and then allowing the equipment to deliver rewarding biofeedback whenever this response is made. Or if you want to provide continuous feedback rather than the discrete form just described, you need a system that will feed back even the smallest of responses to the subject during early sessions but will allow change in the gain or sensitivity during later sessions requiring the subject to make larger and larger responses in order to receive the same rewarding biofeedback.

In conclusion, there are good biofeedback instruments and there are bad biofeedback instruments just as there are good biofeedback books and bad biofeedback books. Caveat emptor!

25

Equipment Suppliers

In Chapter 24 we discussed the various components of a biofeedback system and we mentioned several desirable features of the instruments. If you would like to see a demonstration of numerous biofeedback devices we suggest that you contact one of the companies listed below.

A list of suppliers of biofeedback equipment follows:

Alpha Metrics, 6311 Yucca Street, Los Angeles, CA 90028
Aquarius Electronics, Box 96, Albion, CA 95410
Autogenic Systems, Inc., 809 Allston Way, Berkeley, CA 94710
Bio Behavioral Instruments, PO Box 631, Claremont, CA 91711
Bio-Dyne Corporation, 154 E. Erie, Chicago, IL 60611
Biofeedback Electronics, Inc., PO Box 1491, Monterey, CA 93940
Biofeedback Instruments, 223 Crescent St., Waltham, MA 02154
Biofeedback Research Institute, 6233 Wilshire Blvd., Los Angeles, CA 90048
Biofeedback Systems, Inc., 2736 47th Street, Boulder, CO 80301
Bio-feedback Technology, Inc., 10612A Trask Ave., Garden Grove, CA 92643
BioMonitoring Applications, 270 Madison Ave., Suite 1506, New York, NY 10016
BioScan Corporation, 6842 Westover, Houston, TX 77017
Coulbourn Instruments, Inc., PO Box 2551, Lehigh Valley, PA 18001

Cyborg Corporation, 342 Western Ave., Boston, MA 02135
Edmund Scientific Co., EDSCORP Bldg., Barrington, NJ 08007
Electro Labs, PO Box 2386, Pomona, CA 91766
Electronic Developments, 37 E. Platts Eyot, Lower Sunbury Rd., Hampton, Middlesex TW12 2HF, England
Extended Digital Concepts, PO Box 9161, Berkeley, CA 94709
Harvard Apparatus Co., Inc., 150 Dover Rd., Millis, MA 02054
Huma Tech Industries, 1725 Rogers Ave., San Jose, CA 95112
InnerSpace Unlimited, Beach Road, Ossining, NY 10562
J & J Enterprises, Rt. 8, PO Box 8102, Bainbridge Island, WA 98110
Lawson Electronics, PO Box 711, Poteet, TX 78065
M.O.E., Dept. 6, PO Box 2693, Santa Cruz, CA 95063
Marietta Apparatus Co., 118 Maple St., Marietta, OH 45750
Med Associates, Inc., PO Box 47, East Fairfield, VT 05448
Medical Device Corp., 1555 N. Bellefontaine Street, Indianapolis, IN 46202
Medlab, PO Box 31035, San Francisco, CA 94131
Narco Bio-Systems, Inc., 7651 Airport Blvd., Houston, TX 77017
Neuro Feedback Instruments, 6901 Katherine Ave., Van Nuys, CA 91405
Neuronics, Inc., 104 East Oak, Chicago, IL 60611
Ortec, Inc., Life Science Products, 100 Midland Road, Oak Ridge, TN 37830
Phenomenological Systems, Inc., 72 Otis Street, San Francisco, CA 94103
Quartec, 1662 Doone Road, Columbus, OH 43221
Radio Shack, 2017 W. 7th Street, Forth Worth, TX 76107
Royer-Anderson, 763 LaPara Ave., Palo Alto, CA 94306
Self Control Systems, PO Box 6462, San Diego, CA 92106
Stoelting Co., 1350 S. Kostner Ave., Chicago, IL 60623
Systec, Inc., 5000 Locust St., Lawrence, KA 66044
Terrasyn, Inc., PO Box 975, Longmont, CO 80501
Uniquity, PO Box 990, Venice, CA 90291

Glossary

Adrenal Medulla Portion of the adrenal gland which secretes adrenalin.
Adrenalin Same as epinephrine; speeds up heart, contracts blood vessels, etc.
Airway Resistance The degree of difficulty in breathing.
Alpha Waves Relatively high amplitude brain waves, 8-12 Hz.
Anorexia Abnormal lack of appetite.
Arteriosclerosis Thickening and hardening of the arteries.
Artifact Stray and unwanted electrical signal in a physiological recording.
Asthma Disorder characterized by increased airways resistance caused by constriction in the bronchioles.
Atrial Fibrillation Irregular contraction of the atrium of the heart.
Augmented Sensory Feedback See Biofeedback.
Autogenic Training A method that combines relaxation with imagery in a series of exercises for overall health.
Autonomic Nervous System (ANS) Serves the smooth muscles and glands.
Beta Waves Relatively low amplitude brain waves; 13-25 Hz.
Bile A secretion of the liver which aids in digestion.
Biofeedback Information that we receive about the functioning of our internal organs.
Brain Waves See Electroencephalogram.
Bronchioles Tubes through which air reaches the lungs.
Bruxism Excessive grinding of teeth.
Cardiac Arrhythmias Disorders involving heart rate.
Cardiovascular Refers to the heart and blood vessels.

Carotid Artery Located in neck; carries blood to the brain.

Central Nervous System (CNS) Spinal cord and the brain.

Cerebral Palsy A disorder characterized by paralysis.

Cervical and Lumbar Sympathectomies Surgical interruption of the sympathetic nerves.

Classical Conditioning The repeated pairing of a stimulus to be conditioned with one which already brings about the desired response.

Clinical Significance A change in behavior large enough to be considered a meaningful improvement.

Cognitive Factors Refers to thinking.

Continent Able to control voluntarily feces and/or urine.

Coronary Heart Disease A disorder involving the main artery which supplies blood to the heart muscle.

Cyanosis Skin turning blue from lack of blood (oxygen).

Dexamyl A stimulant sometimes prescribed for obesity.

Diastolic Blood Pressure Lowest pressure recorded from an individual during a cardiac cycle.

Digital Vasomotor Activity Amount of blood in the fingers.

Dorsal Flexion of the Foot Bending back (up) the foot and lifting the toes.

Dumo Breathing A type of breathing produced under internal pressure which claims to allow one to sit in a cold situation without freezing.

Electrodes Small pieces of metal that are attached to the skin in order to record the electrical signals given off by the body.

Electroencephalogram (EEG) Record of the electrical activity of the brain recorded from the skull.

Electromyogram (EMG) Record of the electrical activity of a muscle usually recorded from the surface of the skin.

Endocrine Refers to the endocrine glands which produce important internal secretions.

Epilepsy Disorder of the CNS characterized by convulsions.

Ergotamine Tartrate Drug used to relieve migraine.

Essential Hypertension Disorder characterized by high blood pressure of unknown origin.

External Rectal Sphincter Circular muscle normally under voluntary control which is used in defecating.

Fecal Incontinence Inability to control when defecation takes place.

Feedback See Biofeedback.

Foot-Drop Inability to dorsal flex the foot often resulting from a stroke.

Frontalis Muscle Located in the forehead.

Functional Diarrhea Diarrhea without a known organic cause.

Functional Electrical Stimulation (FES) External electrical stimulation to a muscle.

Galvanic Skin Responses (GSR) A measure of arousal related to the degree of sweating that takes place in the hand.

Gastrointestinal System (G.I.) That part of the digestive system that includes the stomach and intestines.

G.I. Motility Frequency and amplitude of contractions in the gastrointestinal system.

Glycogen A carbohydrate released from the liver.

Hawthorne Effect Individuals producing more because they feel that their superiors are concerned about them.

Homeostasis Tendency for stability in the normal body states of an organism.

Humanistic Psychology A field of psychology which recognizes our human qualities and explores the development of human potential.

Hypertension High blood pressure.

Hz. Abbreviation for Hertz or cycles per second.

Instrumental Conditioning See Operant Conditioning.

Laryngeal Muscle Located in the throat; important in speaking.

Lie Detection An attempt to discriminate between truth telling and lying through the use of physiological recording.

Locus of Control A personality construct which is dependent upon whether the individual perceives his rewards as being contingent upon his own behavior or by chance.

Masseter Muscle Closes the jaws; important in chewing.

Method Actors Express emotions on the stage by thinking of a personal experience that included the desired emotion.

Microvolt One one-millionth of a volt.

Migraine Headaches Severe headaches on one side that are sometimes preceded by visual disturbances.

Morse Code Communication system which depends on various combinations of dots and dashes to form letters.

Motor Units Groups of motor neurons, many of which comprise a muscle.

Muscle Reeducation Refers to the retraining of paralyzed muscles through the use of EMG biofeedback.

Occipital Area of the Brain Part of the cerebral cortex lying at the back of the head.

Operant Conditioning Rewarding of a response.

Orthotic Device A brace.

Parasympathetic Nervous System A branch of the ANS; tends to return an individual to a relaxed state.

Parocysmal Atrial Tachycardia Disorder characterized by a sudden increase in the rate of contraction of the atrium of the heart.

Peripheral Skin Temperature Skin temperature of the hands and feet.

Peroneal Nerve Nerve in leg which controls dorsal flexion of feet.

pH Acid-base balance.

Photocell Transducer Converts amount of light to a change in electrical resistance.

Physiological Responses Refer to any bodily changes, e.g., heart rate.

Pinna Outer part of the ear.

Placebo A medication or treatment given merely to please the patient.

Premature Ventricular Contractions (PVCs) Disorder in which the heart muscle does not contract in a smooth coordinated manner.

Primary Process In Freudian theory, the unconscious is generally associated with primary process thinking which has its goal as wish fulfillment and instinctual discharge.

Proprioceptive Information from muscles, tendons, and joints.

Prosthesis Artificial limb.

Psychophysiology The study of the relationship between behavior and bodily changes, usually in humans.

Psychosomatic Problem Disorder which is brought on or made worse by emotional disturbance.

Pulse Volume (PV) Related to the degree of constriction that takes place in the small blood vessels, usually of the hand.

Raja Yoga "Royal" yoga—emphasizes the development of mental control.

Raynaud's Disease Characterized by severe cold and even pain in the hands and/or feet.

Rectosphincteric Reflex The normal tendency to close the external rectal muscle, and thereby delay defecation, when feces enter the rectum.

Relaxation Response A response said by Herbert Benson to be the main ingredient of many meditative techniques.

Reverie A state of dreamy meditation.

Sensing Device Electrodes or transducers.

Sensorimotor Rhythm A 12-14 Hz. brain wave pattern.

Shaping Technique for teaching a desired response through a series of successive steps.

Signal Conditioners Usually preamplifiers and filters.

Sinus Tachycardia Disorder characterized by rapid heart rate.

Skeletal Muscles Those that move the trunk and limbs.

Smooth Muscles Refers to the muscles found in the blood vessels, gastrointestinal system, heart, etc.

Sociopath An impulsive person who experiences little guilt or anxiety following an improper act.

Somatic Refers to the body.

Spastic Refers to muscle spasm.

Strain-Gage Transducer Sensing device that changes in electrical resistance as a function of the degree to which it is stretched.

Stress Psychological tension or strain.

Stroke Interruption of normal blood supply to the brain usually resulting in partial paralysis.

Successive Approximations See Shaping.

Supraventricular Tachycardia Disorder characterized by rapid contraction of the ventricles of the heart.

Sympathetic Nervous System A branch of the ANS; most active when an individual is aroused.

Systolic Blood Pressure Highest pressure recorded from an individual during a cardiac cycle.

Tension Headache Characterized by unusually high muscle tension in areas near the head.

Thermistor Sensing device which changes in electrical resistance as a function of temperature.

Thermocouple Sensing device which changes in voltage as a function of temperature.

Theta Relatively high amplitude brain waves; 4-7 Hz.

Third Degree Heart Block Interruption of normal electrical conductivity within the heart.

Tic Involuntary, spasmodic contraction of certain muscle fibers, often in the face.

Torticollis (Wryneck) Disorder characterized by twisting of the neck and unnatural position of the head.

Total Respiratory Resistance A measure of how difficult it is for a person to breathe, largely as a function of bronchial constriction.

Trachea Tube extending from the larynx to the bronchi in the chest.

Transcendental Meditation (TM) A technique of meditation as taught by Maharishi Mahesh Yogi. It involves repeating a mantra or sound.

Transducer Converts a physical change into a corresponding electrical output.

Ulcer A sore sometimes found in the inside wall of the small intestine or stomach.

Vasomotor Activity Refers to the degree of vasoconstriction and vasodilation of the small blood vessels.

Velum Soft palate which lies between the oral and nasal cavities.

Vertigo Disorder characterized by dizziness.

Vigilance Alertness, ability to respond to information.

Viscera Internal organs; often thought of as just stomach and intestines.

Wolff-Parkinson-White Syndrome Disorder of the heart characterized by rapid heart beat.

Yoga Means union—in general a set of techniques that seek to place the individual in total contact with the reality around him. These techniques may involve both physical and mental discipline.

Zen A school of Mahayana Buddhism mostly known for simple yet paradoxical teaching methods such as a Koan, e.g., "What was your face before your parents were born?" and instructions to its students that they should "just sit" when meditating.

Notes and References

Chapter 1. What Is Biofeedback

For a very brief introduction to biofeedback we modestly recommend our previous publication—R. M. Stern and W. J. Ray. *Biofeedback and the Control of Internal Bodily Activity.* Homewood, Ill.: Learning Systems, 1975.

1. N. Weiner, cited in L. Birk, ed. *Biofeedback: Behavioral Medicine.* New York: Grune & Stratton, 1973.

2. L. Birk, ed. *Biofeedback: Behavioral Medicine.* New York: Grune & Stratton, 1973.

Chapter 2. Disease and Stress

1. This research is presented and discussed in D. Bakan. *Disease, Pain and Sacrifice.* Boston: Beacon Press, 1968.

2. W. Cannon. *The Wisdom of the Body.* New York: W. W. Norton, 1932.

3. H. Selye. *The Stress of Life.* New York: McGraw-Hill, 1956.

4. L. Edson. "The Dark Secrets of Doctors: Most Things Get Better by Themselves." *New York Times Sunday Magazine.* July 4, 1976.

5. L. Thomas. *Lives of a Cell.* New York: Viking, 1974.

Chapter 3. Biofeedback, Zen, Yoga, TM, Relaxation Response and Autogenic Training

1. R. Wilheim, tr. *The Secret of the Golden Flower.* New York: Harcourt, Brace & World, 1962.
2. E. Green, A. Green, and D. Walters. "Biofeedback for Mind-Body Self Regulation: Healing and Creativity." *Fields within Fields . . . within Fields,* 1972, 5, 131-44.
3. M. A. Wenger, B. K. Bagchi, and B. K. Anand. "Experiments in India on 'Voluntary' Control of the Heart and Pulse." *Circulation,* 1961, 24, 1319-25.
4. B. K. Bagchi and A. Wenger. "Electro-Physiological Correlates of Some Yogi Exercises." *EEG and Clinical Neurophysiology,* 1957, Supplement 7, 132-49.
5. A. Kasamatsu and T. Hirai. "An Electroencephalographic Study of the Zen Meditator (Zazen)." *Folia Psychiatrica et Neurologia Jaoponica,* 1966, 20, 315-36.
6. A. Smith. *Powers of Mind.* New York: Random House, 1975.
7. R. K. Wallace. *The Physiological Effects of Transcendental Meditation* (reprint of dissertation). Los Angeles: MIUPRESS, 1970.
8. H. Benson. *The Relaxation Response.* New York: William Morrow, 1975.
9. J. Schultz and W. Luthe. *Autogenic Training.* New York: Grune & Stratton, 1959. (A recent popular book is by K. Rosa. *You and A.T.* New York: E. P. Dutton, 1973.)
10. F. Edgerton, tr. *The Bhagavad Gita.* New York: Harper & Row, 1964.
11. H. Selye. *The Stress of Life.* New York: McGraw-Hill, 1956.

Chapter 4. Early Scientific Research

1. A general review of Miller's work is found in N. E. Miller. "Learning of Visceral and Glandular Responses." *Science,* 1969, 163, 434-45. A popular discussion of his work is found in G. Jonas. *Visceral Learning.* New York: Viking Press, 1973.
2. G. Ádám. *Interoception and Behavior.* Budapest: Akademiai Kiado, 1967.

3. J. Kamiya. "Operant Control of the EEG Alpha Rhythm and Some of Its Reported Effects on Consciousness." In C. Tart (Ed.), *Altered States of Consciousness.* New York: Wiley, 1969.

4. RMS heard this research described by R. C. Davis in a class at Indiana University in 1960. The results were never published to the best of our knowledge, and we recently tried to obtain more information about the project but failed. We think that this late 1950s project is technically as good as any present-day biofeedback application and include it for that reason.

5. J. V. Basmajian. "Electromyography Comes of Age." *Science,* 1972, 176, 603-9.

6. T. H. Budzynski, J. M. Stoyva, and C. S. Adler. "Feedback-Induced Muscle Relaxation: Application to Tension Headache." *Behavior Therapy and Experimental Psychiatry,* 1970, 1, 205-11.

7. A review of Kimmel's work in this area can be found in H. D. Kimmel. "Instrumental Conditioning of Autonomically Mediated Responses." *American Psychologist,* 1972, 29, 325-35.

8. R. M. Stern and B. Kaplan. "Galvanic Skin Response: Voluntary Control and Externalization." *Journal of Psychosomatic Research,* 1967, 10, 349-53.

9. R. M. Stern and N. L. Lewis. "Ability of Actors to Control Their GSRs and Express Emotions." *Psychophysiology,* 1968, 4, 294-99.

10. P. Simonov, M. N. Valneva, and P. M. Ershov. "Voluntary Regulation of the Galvanic Skin Response." *Voprosy Psikhologii,* 1964, 6, 45-50.

11. D. W. Shearn. "Operant Conditioning of Heart Rate." *Science,* 1962, 137, 530-31.

12. M. Hnatiow and P. J. Lang. "Learned Stabilization of Cardiac Rate." *Psychophysiology,* 1965, 1, 330-36.

13. J. Brener and D. Hothersall. "Heart Rate Control under Conditions of Augmented Sensory Feedback." *Psychophysiology,* 1966, 3, 23-28.

14. D. V. Chalmers and R. M. Stern. "Voluntary Control of Autonomic Responses: External Feedback and Response Specificity." Unpublished manuscript. Penn State University, 1972.

15. G. E. Schwartz. "Voluntary Control of Human Cardiovascular Integration and Differentiation through Feedback and Reward." *Science,* 1972, 175, 90-93.

16. J. H. Stephens, A. H. Harris, and J. V. Brady. "Large Magnitude Heart Rate Changes in Subjects Instructed to Change Their Heart Rates and Given Exteroceptive Feedback." *Psychophysiology,* 1972, 9, 283-85.
17. W. J. Ray. "The Relationship of Locus of Control, Self-Report Measures, and Feedback to the Voluntary Control of Heart Rate." *Psychophysiology,* 1974, 11, 527-34.
18. B. Brown. *New Mind, New Body.* New York: Harper & Row, 1974.

Chapter 5. High Blood Pressure

1. M. Sokolow, D. Werdegar, H. Kain, and A. Hinman. "Relationship between Level of Blood Pressure Measured Casually and by Portable Recorders and Severity of Complications in Essential Hypertension." *Circulation,* 1966, 34, 279-98.
2. The cross-cultural data were supplied by Dr. Paul Baker, Department of Anthropology, Penn State University, University Park, PA.
3. D. Shapiro, B. Tursky, E. Gershon, and M. Stern. "Effects of Feedback and Reinforcement on the Control of Human Systolic Blood Pressure." *Science,* 1969, 163, 588-90.
4. H. Benson, D. Shapiro, B. Tursky, and G. Schwartz. "Decreased Systolic Blood Pressure through Operant Conditioning Techniques in Patients with Essential Hypertension." *Science,* 1971, 173, 740-42.
5. The last time we heard this story was at the Society for Psychophysiological Research meeting in Toronto in 1975.
6. A general statement of Miller's work by Miller appears in his chapter on visceral learning in *Comprehensive Textbook of Psychiatry/II.* Volume 1. Baltimore: Williams & Wilkins, 1975.
7. D. Shapiro and R. Surwit. "Learned Control of Physiological Functioning and Disease." In H. Leitenberg, ed. *Handbook of Behavior Modification and Behavior Therapy.* New York: Prentice Hall, 1976.
8. D. Kristt and B. T. Engel. "Learned Control of Blood Pressure in Patients with High Blood Pressure." *Circulation,* 1975, 51, 370-78.

Chapter 6. Heart Rate Disorders

1. An interesting and short history of heart disease dating back to Aristotle is found in C. McMahon. "The Psychosomatic Approach to Heart Disease: A Study in Premodern Medicine." *Chest,* 1976, 69, 531-37.

2. See any medical physiology textbook for more information about the physiology of heart functioning. See also P. Obrist, A. H. Black, J. Brener, and L. V. DiCara (eds.), *Cardiovascular Psychophysiology.* Chicago: Aldine, 1974.

3. T. Weiss and B. T. Engel. "Operant Conditioning of Heart Rate in Patients with Premature Ventricular Contraction." *Psychosomatic Medicine,* 1971, 33, 301-21.

4. See the Engel and Bleecker chapter in Obrist, Black, Brener and DiCara— Note 2 above.

Chapter 7. Raynaud's Disease: Cold Hands or Feet

1. B. Mittelmann and H. G. Wolff. "Affective States and Skin Temperature: Experimental Study of Subjects with 'Cold Hands' and Raynaud's Syndrome." *Psychosomatic Medicine,* 1939, 1, 271-92.

2. M. I. Lisina. "The Role of Orientation in the Transformation of Involuntary into Voluntary Reactions." In L. G. Voronin et al. (Eds.), *Orienting Reflex and Exploratory Behavior.* Washington: American Psychological Association, 1965 (in English). C. Snyder and M. Noble. "Operant Conditioning of Vasoconstriction." *Journal of Experimental Psychology,* 1968, 77, 263-68.

3. D. Shapiro and R. Surwit. "Learned Control of Physiological Functioning and Disease." In H. Leitenberg (Ed.), *Handbook of Behavior Modification and Behavior Therapy.* New York: Prentice Hall, 1976.

4. E. Taub. "Self-Regulation of Human Tissue Temperature." In G. E. Schwartz and J. Beatty (Eds.), *Biofeedback: Theory and Research.* New York: Academic Press, 1977.

5. E. Peper. This case study was presented at the American Psychological Association meeting, 1974.

Chapter 8. Asthma

1. W. B. Sherman. *Hypersensitivity.* Philadelphia: W. B. Saunders, 1968.

2. Two journals, *Psychosomatic Medicine* and *Journal of Psychosomatic Research,* often have articles on the psychological aspects of asthma.

3. This report is from the clinical files of WJR. A study by Straker and Tamerin at a boys' camp lends support to the inhibition of aggression hypothesis. N. Straker and J. Tamerin. "Aggression and Childhood Asthma." *Journal of Psychosomatic Research,* 1974, 18, 131-35.

4. A good summary of studies dealing with psychological data in asthma may be found in D. Graham's chapter on Psychosomatic Medicine which appeared in N. Greenfield and R. Sternback (Eds.), *Handbook of Psychophysiology*. New York: Holt, Rinehart & Winston, 1972.

5. R. Levenson, S. Manuck, H. Strupp, G. Blackwood, and J. Snell. "A Biofeedback Technique for Bronchial Asthma." *Proceedings of the Biofeedback Research Society*, 1974 (Abstract).

6. L. Vachon and E. Rich. "Visceral Learning in Asthma." *Psychosomatic Medicine*, 1976, 38, 122-30.

7. G. Feldman. "The Effect of Biofeedback Training on Respiratory Resistance of Asthmatic Children." *Psychosomatic Medicine*, 1976, 38, 27-34.

8. A. Tal and D. Miklich. "Emotionally Induced Decreases in Pulmonary Flow Rates in Asthmatic Children." *Psychosomatic Medicine*, 1976, 38, 190-200.

9. A. Sirota and M. Mahoney. "Relaxing on Cue: The Self-Regulation of Asthma." *Journal of Behavior Therapy and Experimental Psychiatry*, 1974, 5, 65-66.

10. M. Davis, D. Saunders, T. Creer, and H. Chai. "Relaxation Training Facilitated by Biofeedback Apparatus as a Supplemental Treatment in Bronchial Asthma." *Journal of Psychosomatic Research*, 1973, 17, 121-28.

Chapter 9. Epilepsy

1. M. B. Sterman, R. C. Howe, and L. R. MacDonald. "Facilitation of Spindle-Burst Sleep by Conditioning of Electroencephalographic Activity While Awake." *Science*, 1970, 167, 1145-48.

2. M. B. Sterman and L. Friar. "Suppression of Seizures in an Epileptic Following Sensorimotor EEG Feedback Training." *Electroencephalography and Clinical Neurophysiology*, 1972, 33, 89-95.

3. W. W. Finley, H. Smith, and M. Etherton. "Reduction of Seizures and Normalization of the EEG in a Severe Epileptic Following Sensorimotor Biofeedback Training: Preliminary Study." *Biological Psychology*, 1975, 2, 189-203.

4. A. R. Seifert and J. F. Lubar. "Reduction of Epileptic Seizures through EEG Biofeedback Training." *Biological Psychology*, 1975, 3, 157-84.

5. J. Lubar and W. W. Bahler. "Behavioral Management of Epileptic Seizures

Following EEG Biofeedback Training of the Sensorimotor Rhythm." *Biofeedback and Self-Regulation*, 1976, 1, 77-104.

6. For a report that did not show biofeedback change, see B. Kaplan. "Biofeedback in Epileptics: Equivocal Relationship of Reinforced EEG Frequency to Seizure Reduction." *Epilepsia*, 1975, 16, 477-85.

Chapter 10. Tension Headache

1. D. Bakal. "Headache: A Biopsychological Perspective." *Psychological Bulletin*, 1975, 82, 369-82.

2. R. B. Malmo. *On Emotions, Needs, and Our Archaic Brain.* New York: Holt, Rinehart & Winston, 1975.

3. T. Budzynski, J. Stoyva, and C. Adler. "Feedback-Induced Muscle Relaxation: Application to Tension Headache." *Journal of Behavior Therapy and Experimental Psychiatry*, 1970, 1, 205-11.

4. T. Budzynski, J. Stoyva, C. Adler, and D. Mullaney. "EMG Biofeedback and Tension Headache: A Controlled Outcome Study." *Psychosomatic Medicine*, 1973, 35, 484-96.

5. One brief but good review of the placebo effect is found in A. Shapiro. "Contribution to a History of the Placebo Effect." *Behavioral Science*, 1960, 5, 109-35.

6. This quotation is from Chapter 87, Verses 5-7 of *The Gospel According to Thomas* translated by A. Guillaumont, H. Ch. Puech, G. Quispel, W. Till and Yassah 'Abd Al Masih. New York: Harper & Row, 1959.

7. The original study was reported in F. J. Roethlisberger and W. J. Dickson. *Management and the Worker.* Cambridge, Mass.: Harvard University Press, 1939. It is also discussed in most industrial psychology texts.

Chapter 11. Migraine Headaches

1. Quote is from O. Sacks. *Migraine.* Berkeley: University of California Press, 1970.

2. Ad Hoc Committee on Classification of Headache. "Classification of Headache." *Journal of the American Medical Association*, 1962, 179, 717-18.

3. J. Sargent, E. Green, and E. D. Walters. "The Use of Autogenic Feedback Training in a Pilot Study of Migraine and Tension Headaches." *Headache*, 1972, 12, 120-24.

4. E. Peper and E. Grossman. "Thermal Biofeedback Training in Children with Headaches." Presented at the Biofeedback Research Society Meeting, 1974.

5. S. Diamond and M. Franklin. "Biofeedback—Choice of Treatment in Childhood Migraine." Presented at the Biofeedback Research Society meeting, 1974.

6. L. Friar and J. Beatty. "Migraine: Management by Trained Control of Vasoconstriction." *Journal of Consulting and Clinical Psychology*, 1976, 44, 46-53.

Chapter 12. Stomach and Intestinal Disorders

1. R. M. Stern and J. D. Higgins. "Perceived Somatic Reactions to Stress: Sex, Age, and Familial Occurrence." *Journal of Psychosomatic Research*, 1969, 13, 77-82.

2. Technically speaking, the g.i. system extends from the lips to the anus, but we commonly think of it as including just stomach and intestines.

3. For a report describing how bodily reactions to stress are labeled in different societies see G. M. Guthrie, A. Verstraete, M. Deines, and R. M. Stern. "Symptoms of Stress in Four Societies." *Journal of Social Psychology*, 1975, 95, 165-72.

4. The famous physiologist Cannon used the balloon method of recording stomach motility to arrive at his conclusions concerning the relationship between stomach contractions and feelings of hunger. W. B. Cannon, A. L. Washburn. "An Explanation of Hunger." *American Journal of Physiology*, 1912, 29, 441-54. Several lines of evidence have since demonstrated that this relation is not causal.

5. R. C. Davis, L. Garafalo, and F. Gault. "An Exploration of Abdominal Potentials." *Journal of Comparative and Physiological Psychology*, 1957, 50, 519-23. Davis used the balloon method to compare his surface recording technique to the more widely accepted method. A more recent description of the surface recording technique by R. W. Russell and R. M. Stern appears in P. Venables and I. Martin (Eds.), *A Manual of Psychophysiological Methods*. Amsterdam: North-Holland, 1967.

6. C. W. Deckner, J. T. Hill, and J. R. Bourne. "Shaping of Human Gastric Motility." Paper presented at the meeting of the American Psychological Association, 1972.

7. M. Harris. "Symptom-Related Differences in the Biofeedback Per-

formances of Psychosomatic Patients." Dissertation conducted in the Psychology Department at The Pennsylvania State University.

8. S. Furman. "Intestinal Biofeedback in Functional Diarrhea: A Preliminary Report." *Journal of Behavior Therapy and Experimental Psychiatry,* 1974, 4, 317-21.

9. B. T. Engel, P. Nikoomanash, and M. M. Schuster. "Operant Conditioning of Rectosphincteric Responses in the Treatment of Fecal Incontinence." *New England Journal of Medicine,* 1974, 290, 646-49. These investigators also recorded the degree of contraction of the interior sphincter; the interested reader is referred to the article for details.

10. P. J. Gorman and J. Kamiya. "Biofeedback Training of Stomach pH." Paper presented at the Western Psychological Association meeting, 1972.

    W. E. Whitehead, P. F. Renault, and I. Goldiamond. "Modification of Human Gastric Acid Secretion with Operant Conditioning Procedures." *Journal of Applied Behavior Analysis,* 1975, 8, 147-51.

11. P. R. Welgan. "Learned Control of Gastric Acid Secretions in Ulcer Patients." *Psychosomatic Medicine,* 1974, 36, 411-19.

Chapter 13. Pain

1. This particular study looking at instructions is by B. Blitz and A. J. Dinnerstein. "Role of Attentional Focus in Pain Perception." *Journal of Abnormal Psychology,* 1971, 77, 42-45.

2. K. Pelletier and E. Peper. "Developing a Biofeedback Model: Alpha EEG Feedback as a Means for Pain Control." Unpublished manuscript.

3. L. Gannon and R. Sternbach. "Alpha Enhancement as a Treatment for Pain: A Case Study." *Journal of Behavior Therapy and Experimental Psychology,* 1971, 2, 209-13.

4. B. K. Anand, G. S. Chhina, and B. Singh. "Some Aspects of Electroencephalographic Studies in Yogis." *EEG and Clinical Neurophysiology,* 1961, 13, 452-56.

5. R. Melzack and C. Perry. "Self-Regulation of Pain." *Experimental Neurology,* 1975, 46, 452-69. A more informal report was published in *Psychology Today,* July, 1975.

6. Brief write-ups can be found in *Ob-Gyn Observer,* June-July 1975 (con-

cerning labor and biofeedback); *Bestways*, July 1975 (the Casa Colina Hospital in Pomona, California program for pain).

Chapter 14. Bruxism: Excessive Teeth Grinding

1. J. D. Rugh and W. K. Solberg. "Electromyographic Studies of Bruxist Behavior before and during Treatment." *Canadian Dental Association Journal*, 1975, 3, 56-59.

2. R. F. Heller and H. R. Strong. "Controlling Bruxism through Automated Aversive Conditioning." *Behaviour Research and Therapy*, 1973, 11, 327-29.

3. A. J. Cannistraci. *Voluntary Stress Release and Behavior Therapy in the Treatment of Clenching and Bruxism.* Tape T5. Biomonitoring Applications, N.Y.

Chapter 15. Muscle Reeducation

1. For a more complete discussion of the anatomy and physiology of motor units, see J. V. Basmajian. *Muscles Alive: Their Functions Revealed by Electromyography.* Baltimore: Williams and Wilkins, 1974.

2. A. A. Marinacci. *Applied Electromyography.* Philadelphia: Lea and Febiger, 1968.

3. S. M. Owen, H. Toomim, and L. P. Taylor. *Biofeedback in Neuromuscular Re-Education.* Los Angeles: Biofeedback Research Institute, 1975. The book contains an introduction to neuromuscular disorders and examples of the application of EMG biofeedback. Helpful diagrams and a glossary are included.

4. J. V. Basmajian, C. G. Kukulka, M. G. Narayan, and K. Takebe. "Biofeedback Treatment of Foot-Drop after Stroke Compared with Standard Rehabilitation Technique: Effects on Voluntary Control and Strength." *Archives of Physical Medicine and Rehabilitation*, 1975, 56, 231-36.

5. D. Fish, N. Mayer, and R. Herman. "Biofeedback" (Letter to the Editor). *Archives of Physical Medicine and Rehabilitation*, 1976, 57, 152.

6. A summary of their findings can be found in *Progress Report #4*, the Rehabilitation Engineering Center, Moss Rehabilitation Hospital, Philadelphia, PA, 1975.

7. In a very recent article (E. Peper and J. A. Robertson. "Biofeedback Use

of Common Objects: The Bathroom Scale in Physical Therapy." *Biofeedback and Self-Regulation,* 1976, 2, 237-40) the use of the bathroom scale to achieve the same goals is discussed.
8. W. W. Finley, C. Niman, J. Standley, and R. Wansley. "Frontal EMG Biofeedback Training of Cerebral Palsy Children." Paper presented at the Biofeedback Research Society meeting, 1976.

Chapter 16. Control of Paralyzed or Artificial Limbs

Much of the research described in this chapter and some of the work described in the last chapter has been supported by the Rehabilitation Engineering Program of the Rehabilitation Services Administration, U.S. Department of Health, Education and Welfare.

1. W. T. Liberson, H. J. Holmquist, D. Scott, and M. Dow. "Functional Electrotherapy: Stimulation of the Peroneal Nerve Synchronized with the Swing Phase of the Gait of Hemiplegic Patients." *Archives of Physical Medicine and Rehabilitation,* 1961, 42, 101.
2. M. L. Moe and J. T. Schwartz. "Ocular Control of the Rancho Electric Arm." In M. M. Gavrilovic and A. B. Wilson, Jr. (Eds.). *Advances in External Control of Human Extremities.* Belgrade: Yugoslav Committee for Electronics and Automation, 1973.
3. Children whose mothers took the drug thalidomide while they were pregnant. Many of these children were born without arms or legs or with severely deformed and/or stunted arms or legs.

Chapter 17. Teaching Deaf Children to Speak

Much of the material in this chapter was adapted from R. S. Nickerson. *Speech Training and Speech Reception Aids for the Deaf.* Report No. 2980. Cambridge, Mass.: Bolt Beranek and Newman, Inc., 1975.

1. This research is being carried out at the Smith Kettlewell Institute of Visual Sciences, San Francisco, California.
2. Cybernetics Research Institute, Inc., Washington, D.C.
3. A. Boothroyd. Comments in Chapter 3 of R. E. Stark (Ed.). *Sensory Capabilities of Hearing-Impaired Children.* Baltimore: University Park Press, 1974.

Chapter 18. Stuttering

1. G. Wyatt. *Language Learning and Communication Disorders in Children.* New York: The Free Press, 1969.

2. W. Johnson et al. *The Onset of Stuttering.* Minneapolis: University of Minnesota Press, 1959.

3. H. Gregory. *Stuttering: Differential Evaluation and Therapy.* Indianapolis: Bobbs-Merrill, 1973.

4. J. R. LeVee, M. J. Cohen, and W. H. Rickles. "Electromyographic Biofeedback for Relief of Tension in the Facial and Throat Muscles of a Woodwind Musician." *Biofeedback and Self-Regulation,* 1976, 1, 113-20.

5. R. Hanna, F. Wilfling, and B. McNeill. "A Biofeedback Treatment for Stuttering." *Journal of Speech and Hearing Disorders,* 1975, 40, 270-73.

6. F. Myers. "Physiological Correlates of Speech for Stutterers and Nonstutterers." Dissertation conducted in the Speech Pathology and Psychology Departments at Penn State University, 1976.

7. B. Guitar. "Reduction of Stuttering Frequency Using Analog Electromyographic Feedback." *Journal of Speech and Hearing Research,* 1975, 18, 672-85.

Chapter 19. Alertness

1. This story may be apocryphal but is included because we wrote this chapter during the bicentennial year.

2. Cited by J. L. Kennedy.

3. J. L. Kennedy. Some practical problems of the alertness indicator. In W. F. Floyd and A. T. Welford (Eds.), *Fatigue.* London: Lewis, 1953.

4. J. F. O'Hanlon. *Vigilance, The Plasma Catecholamines and Related Biochemical and Physiological Variables.* Technical Report 787-2. Goleta, California: Human Factors Research, 1970.

5. J. Beatty, A. Greenberg, W. P. Deibler, and J. F. O'Hanlon. "Operant Control of Occipital Theta Rhythm Affects Performance in a Radar Monitoring Task." *Science,* 1974, 183, 871-73.

6. J. F. O'Hanlon. *Heart Rate Variability: A New Index of Driver Alertness/Fatigue.* Technical Report No. 1712-1. Goleta, California: Human Factors Research, 1971.

Chapter 20. Lie Detection

Lie detection is big business in this country. Its supporters point out its potential for separating true statements from lies and its detractors consider it snooping and an infringement upon individual privacy. This is not the place to go into the pros and cons of this complex issue. However, after recently reviewing the literature in this field (R. M. Stern and T. Watanabe. "A Selected Bibliography of 'Polygraph' Detection of Deception." *Journal Supplement Abstract Service,* 1972, 2, 134) we concluded that what was needed was more research on the reliability and validity of the more conventional lie detection.

1. A report based upon this research is nearing completion. The study was conducted by J. P. Breen, T. Watanabe, and R. M. Stern.

2. S. Valins. "Cognitive Effects of False Heart Rate Feedback." *Journal of Personality and Social Psychology,* 1966, 4, 400-408.

3. RMS assisted with this research at Indiana University. A report describing it has appeared: N. Worrell. "Differential GSR Conditioning of True and False Decisions." *Journal of Experimental Psychology,* 1970, 86, 13-19.

4. R. M. Stern and C. D. Herrick. "The Effects of Nonveridical Heart Rate Feedback in a Simulated Lie Detection Situation." Unpublished manuscript, Psychology Department, Penn State University, 1968.

Chapter 21. Creativity and the Human Potential

1. A. Maslow. *The Farther Reaches of Human Nature.* New York: Viking Press, 1971.

2. J. Hardt, B. Timmons, C. Yeager, and J. Kamiya. "Studying Power and Coherence Relationships in 6-Channel EEGs: A McLuhanistic Technique Applied to Zen Meditation." Paper presented at the Biofeedback Research Society meeting, 1976.

3. A good introduction to this area is R. Ornstein. *The Psychology of Consciousness.* New York: Penguin Books, 1972.

4. D. Galin. "Implications for Psychiatry of Left and Right Cerebral Specialization: A Neurophysiological Context for Unconscious Processes." *Archives of General Psychiatry,* 1974, 31, 572-83.

5. W. J. Ray, A. W. Frediani, and D. Harman. "Self-Regulation of Hemispheric Asymmetry." *Biofeedback and Self-Regulation,* 1977, 2.

6. T. Budzynski. "Biofeedback and the Twilight States of Consciousness,"

in G. Schwartz and D. Shapiro (Eds.), *Consciousness and Self-Regulation*. New York: Plenum, 1976.

7. E. Green, A. Green, and E. D. Walters. "Voluntary Control of Internal States: Psychological and Physiological." *The Journal of Transpersonal Psychology*, 1970, 1, 1–26. A more recent report was given at the Biofeedback Research Society meeting, 1974.

Chapter 22. Summing Up

1. E. Peper. "Understanding Problems in Research, Education, and Clinical Biofeedback Training: An Experiential Analogy—Urination." *Perspectives in Biology and Medicine*, 1977.

2. W. J. Ray, J. M. Raczynski, T. Rogers, and W. H. Kimball. *Evaluation of Clinical Biofeedback*. New York: Plenum, 1979.

   J. V. Basmajian, ed. *Biofeedback, Principle and Practice for Clinicians*. Baltimore: Williams and Wilkins, 1979.

3. M. T. Orne. "The efficacy of biofeedback therapy." *Annual Review of Medicine*, 1979, 30, 489–503.

   N. E. Miller. "Biofeedback and visceral learning." *Annual Review of Psychology*, 1978, 29, 373–404.

   The December 1978 issue of the journal *Biofeedback and Self-Regulation* is devoted to the evaluation question in relation to specific disorders.

Chapter 24. Instruments Used To Do Biofeedback

A good general textbook which discusses pertinent applications of electronics is T. N. Cornsweet. *The Design of Electric Circuits in the Behavioral Sciences*. New York: Wiley, 1963. Two recent articles which discuss biofeedback apparatus are R. L. Schwitzgebel and J. D. Rugh. "Of Bread, Circuses and Alpha Machines." *American Psychologist*, 1975, 30, 363–70.

D. A. Paskewitz. "Biofeedback Instrumentation: Soldering Closed the Loop." *American Psychologist*, 1975, 30, 371–78.

1. A list of equipment suppliers is provided in Chapter 25.

2. For the person interested in a general introduction to recording bodily responses we would recommend R. M. Stern, W. J. Ray, & C. M. Davis, *Psychophysiological Recording*. New York: Oxford University Press, 1980 (forthcoming); and J. Hassett, *A Primer of Psychophysiology*. San Francisco: Freeman, 1978.

3. Technically, good electrode contact means relatively low resistance in the neighborhood of 5,000 ohms between the electrodes and the skin.
4. Other related terms that you may see in the literature are blood volume and plethysmograph.

Chapter 25. Equipment Suppliers

Prices and products are changing so rapidly that we decided not to include them. In the following article, prices are listed as of summer, 1974: J. D. Rugh and R. L. Schwitzgebel. "Biofeedback Apparatus: List of Suppliers." *Behavior Therapy,* 1975, 6, 238–40.

Index

A

Adrenal medulla, 10
Adrenalin, 10
Alpha waves
  biofeedback and, 33-35, 89-94
  blocking of, 34, 89-90
  bruxism and, 98
  creativity and, 144-45
  defined, 31-32
  development of, 33-34
  hypnosis and, 91-92
  illustration of, 32
  meditation and, 18-19, 34
  pain and, 87, 89-92
  relaxation and, 34-35
Arteriosclerosis, 46
Artificial limb; *see* Prosthetic device
Asthma
  causes of, 61-62
  defined, 61
  factors influencing, 64
  psychological factors and, 62-63
  respiratory resistance and, 63-64
  treatment of, using
    biofeedback, 63-64
    medication, 61, 64
    psychotherapy, 63
    relaxation, 64
Atrial fibrillation, 17
Autogenic training
  common features of, 24
  definition of, 22
  hypertension and, 50
  method of, 23
  migraine headache and, 77-79

Autonomic nervous system (ANS), the
  lie detection and, 133-37
  responses of, 30-31, 57
  voluntary control of, 29-30, 57, 134

B

Beta waves, 31-32
Biofeedback
  annuals on, 160
  aspects of, 14
  associations for, 159
  books on, 159-60
  children treated with, 35-36, 63-64, 77-78, 104-5, 114-18
  clinical applications of; *see specific disorders*
  common features of, 24
  computers and, 63, 110, 115-18
  defined, 5
  drugs versus, 52-55
  early research on, 30-42
  equipment for, 162-71
  films about, 161
  individual responsibility and, 153
  journals on, 159
  lie detection and, 134-39
  problems with, 149-52
  skill training and, 59
  tapes on, 160
  treatment using, for changes in
    airway resistance, 63-64
    blood pressure, 48-51
    brain waves, 33-35, 67-69, 89-92, 127, 130-31, 144-45

193

Biofeedback—*Cont.*
  treatment using, for changes in—*Cont.*
    galvanic skin response, 29, 37-39, 135-36
    gastrointestinal motility, 82-85
    gastrointestinal secretion, 85-86
    heart rate, 30-31, 39-42, 52-55, 135-39
    muscle activity, 35-37, 72-75, 95-99, 101-12, 121-25
    skin temperature (blood flow), 57-60, 77-79
    speech, 115-18
Blood
  flow, related to skin temperature, 57-58, 78-79
  sugar, 10
Blood pressure
  age and, 46
  cardiovascular changes and, 3-4
  control of, with
    biofeedback, 48-51
    relaxation response, 21
  diastolic, 48, 50
  environment and, 41
  heart rate and, 41
  high; *see* Hypertension
  lie detection and, 133
  measurement of, 45-46
  psychological factors and, 45-46
  systolic, 48-51
Brain, the
  electrical activity of; *see* Electroencephalogram (EEG), the
  hemispheres of, 143-44
  occipital area of, 130
  pleasure center of, 30-31
  positive stimulation of, 66-67
Brain waves; *see also types of brain waves*
  alertness and, 127-28
  electroencephalographic measurement of, 31-35
  bruxism and, 98
  control of, with
    biofeedback, 33-35, 89-92
    meditation, 18-19, 142-43
  creativity and, 142-45
  pain and, 89-92
Bronchioles, 61
Bruxism
  biofeedback for, 96-99, 151
  defined, 95
  masseter muscle and, 95, 97-98
  nocturnal, 95-99, 151

C

Cardiac arrhythmias, 52-55; *see also specific types*
Central nervous system (CNS), 29, 37, 154
Cerebral palsy, 104-5
Cerebral vascular accident; *see* Stroke
Classical conditioning, 30
Coronary heart disease, 46, 53

D

Digital vasomotor activity; *see* Blood, flow, related to skin temperature
Disease; *see also specific diseases*
  communicable, 9
  communication and, 12-13
  new conceptions of, 140-42
  paradoxes of, 8-9
  stress and, 9

E

Electrocardiogram, 17
Electrodes
  contact of, 163-64
  defined, 163
  EEG, 31
  EMG, 35, 72
  gastrointestinal (surface), 82
  GSR, 135
  pH, 85
  phony, 138
Electroencephalogram (EEG), the
  brain waves measured by, 31, 66, 127-28, 130-31
  changes in, with
    biofeedback, 33-35
    meditation, 19-20, 142-43
  pain and, 87, 89-92
  patterns of, 32, 128
  spindle burst activity and, 67
Electromyogram (EMG), the
  alertness and, 128-30
  biofeedback and, 35-37, 71-74, 93, 95-99, 101-6, 116, 124
  defined, 35
  foot-drop and, 109-10
  pain and, 87, 93
  prosthetic devices controlled by, 110-12
  stuttering and, 122-24
Epilepsy
  causes of, 66
  defined, 66
  psychological features of, 69
  seizures accompanying, 65-66

Epilepsy—*Cont.*
  sensorimotor rhythm and, 66-69
  treatment of, with
    biofeedback, 67-69
    medication, 66, 68-69
Ergotamine tartrate, 78
Essential hypertension, 47, 49-51; *see also* Hypertension
External rectal sphincter, 84; *see also* Gastrointestinal system (g.i.), the

F

Fecal incontinence, 83-85; *see also* Gastrointestinal system (g.i.), the
Feedback
  auditory, 41, 48, 58, 68, 72-74, 82-83, 85, 95, 97, 104, 114, 122, 130
  continuous, 39, 63, 169
  defined, 3
  devices, 113-14; *see also specific devices*
  electrical; *see* Functional electrical stimulation
  false, 73-74, 136-39
  importance of, 36-39
  lie detection and, 134-39
  monetary, 49, 68, 138
  nonspecific, 79, 98
  removal of, 39
  shaping and, 37, 54, 84, 99, 168-69
  tactile, 113-14
  verbal, 83-84
  visual, 36, 37-41, 48, 53-54, 58, 63, 67-68, 82-83, 85, 115-18
Foot-drop; *see also* Cerebral palsy *and* Stroke
  defined, 102
  dorsal flexion and, 102, 109
  treatment for, using
    EMG biofeedback, 109-10, 151
    functional electrical stimulation, 107-9
    muscle reeducation, 102-4, 107
    orthotic device, 110
Frontalis muscle; *see* Muscle, frontalis
Functional diarrhea, 83; *see also* Gastrointestinal system (g.i.), the
Functional electrical stimulation, 107-10

G

Galvanic skin response (GSR), the
  control of, with
    biofeedback, 29, 37-39, 93
    meditation, 18
  defined, 37

Galvanic skin response—*Cont.*
  heart rate and, 40-42
  lie detection and, 135-39
  personality and, 41-42
Gastrointestinal system (g.i.), the
  disorders of
    diarrhea, 83
    fecal incontinence, 83-85
    migraines and, 82-83
    ulcers, 85-86
  pain, 80-81
  processes in
    motility
      biofeedback of, 82-85
      recording of, 81-82
      rectosphincteric response and, 84
    secretion
      biofeedback of, 85-86
      gastric pH (acidity) and, 85
Glycogen, 10

H

Headache
  categories of, 70
  migraine
    cause of, 76-77
    classical, 78
    defined, 76-77
    g.i. distress and, 82-83
    treatment of, with
      biofeedback, 77-79, 153
      medication, 76, 78
    pain due to, 90
  tension
    cause of, 70
    measurement of, 71-72
    psychological aspects of, 70, 72
    treatment of, with
      biofeedback, 72-75
      medication, 70
      placebo, 73-74
Heart, the; *see also specific disorders*
  disorders of, 52-55
  function of, 52
Heart beats
  fibrillation of, 17
  irregular; *see* Cardiac arrhythmias
  palpitation of, 5
  sino-atrial node and, 52-53
  stress and, 10
Heart rate
  alertness and, 131-32
  blood pressure and, 41
  false feedback of, 136-39

Heart rate—*Cont.*
  galvanic skin response and, 40
  lie detection and, 133, 135-39
  locus of control and, 41-42
  premature ventricular contractions and, 53-54
  variability, 53-54, 131
  voluntary control of, with
    biofeedback, 30-31, 39-42, 53
    meditation, 15-18, 20
Homeostasis, 10-11
Humanistic psychology, 141-42
Hypertension (high blood pressure)
  activity and, 47
  age and, 46
  anxiety and, 45
  arteriosclerosis and, 46
  causes of, 46-47
  city life and, 47
  coronary heart disease and, 46
  diet and, 46-47
  environment and, 46
  essential, 47, 49-51
  measurement of, 45, 48
  medication for, 47
  stress and, 45, 47
  stroke and, 46
  treatment of, with
    biofeedback, 48-51
    meditation, 47
    relaxation response, 47

I

Instrumental conditioning; *see* Operant conditioning
Interactions, 12
Intestines; *see* Gastrointestinal system (g.i.), the

L

Laryngeal muscle; *see* Muscle, laryngeal
Lie detection, 133-39
Locus of control, 41-42

M

Mantra, 20
Meditation; *see also types of meditation*
  common features of, 24
  definition of, 15
  physiological changes with, 15-21, 34, 142-43
Migraines; *see* Headache, migraine
Motor units
  active, 101, 105
  control of, with biofeedback, 101-6
  defined, 36, 100

Motor units—*Cont.*
  latent, 101
Muscle; *see also specific muscular disturbances*
  electrical activity of, 35-37, 71-74
  frontalis (forehead), 72-74, 121-22, 130
  intestinal, 80
  laryngeal, 122-25
  masseter, 95
  paralysis of, 101, 104, 107-10
  potentials, 36, 98, 122, 128-30
  relaxation of, 36-37, 72, 93
  skeletal, 29-30
  stomach, 80
  tension in, 14, 36-37, 70-75, 95-99, 121-25
Muscle reeducation
  biofeedback for, 101-4, 107
  defined, 100-101
  spinal cord injury and, 101-2

O

Operant conditioning
  defined, 30, 66
  GSR and, 37
  heart rate and, 39
  sensorimotor rhythm and, 66-67
  shaping and, 168-69
Orthotic device, 110

P

Pain
  alpha waves and, 89-92
  biofeedback control of, 89-94
  childbirth, 93
  chronic back, 93
  factors in reduction of, 92
  gastrointestinal, 80-81
  headache, 90
  hypnosis and, 91-92
Parasympathetic nervous system, 40
Parocsymal atrial tachycardia, 55
Peroneal nerve, 109
Physiological functioning; *see also specific functions*
  cognitive style and, 42
  control of, with
    biofeedback; *see* Biofeedback
    meditation; *see* Meditation
  discrimination of, 55
  stuttering and, 124
Placebo, 73-75
Poliomyelitis, 35-36, 105
Premature ventricular contractions (PVC), 53-55
Proprioception, 101-2

Prosthetic device, 110-12
Psychosomatic disorders; *see also specific disorders*
  defined, 14
  emotional factors in, 59
Pulse volume, 79

R

Raja yoga, 90
Raynaud's disease, 56-60
Relaxation response (Benson), 20-22
Respiration rate, 18, 20-21
Response specificity, 40

S

Salivation, 29-31
Semantic conditioning, 137
Sensorimotor rhythm, 66-69; *see also* Epilepsy
Shaping, 37, 54, 84, 99, 151, 168-69
Sinus tachycardia, 54
Skin temperature
  biofeedback of, 57-60, 77-78
  blood flow and, 57-58, 78-79
  g.i. distress and, 82-83
  migraine headaches and, 77-78
  Raynaud's disease and, 56-57
  thermal feedback and, 59
Sociopathy, 41
Spastic, 102, 106; *see also* Stroke
Speech, 113-18
Stomach; *see* Gastrointestinal system (g.i.), the
Stress
  behavioral changes accompanying, 12
  disease and, 8-13
  emotional, 11, 50
  g.i. disorders and, 80
  hypertension and, 45
  innate patterns of, 21
  physical, 12, 25
  physiological changes accompanying, 21
  psychological, 25
  stuttering and, 120
Stroke
  defined, 102
  hypertension and, 46, 50
  treatment of, with
    biofeedback, 102-4, 107

Stroke—*Cont.*
  treatment of, with—*Cont.*
    physical therapy, 103
Stuttering
  features of, 119-20
  muscle tension and, 122-25
  treatment of, with
    biofeedback, 121-25
    medication, 121
    psychotherapy, 121-22
Successive approximations, 168; *see also* Shaping
Supraventricular tachycardia, 54
Sympathectomies, 58
Sympathetic nervous system, 10, 40

T

Theraveda meditation, 15
Theta waves
  alertness and, 130-31
  control of, with
    biofeedback, 89
    Zen meditation, 19
  creativity and, 145
  defined, 32
  illustration of, 32
  pain and, 89
Tic, 120
Torticollis, 105-6
Trachea, 61
Transcendental Meditation (T.M.), 19-20
Transducers, 164

U

Ulcers
  defined, 11
  treatment of, 85-86
Ultrasonic device, 132

V-Z

Vasomotor activity, 124
Vigilance, 126-32
Voluntary control; *see* Biofeedback *and* Meditation
Wolff-Parkinson-White syndrome, 55
Yoga
  control of pain with, 89-90
  physiological changes accompanying, 15-19
Zen meditation, 19, 142-43